# A NEW SONG
## in the South

# A NEW SONG
# in the South

The Story of the

BILLY GRAHAM
Greenville, S.C., Crusade

LEWIS F. BRABHAM

*Introduction by Billy Graham*

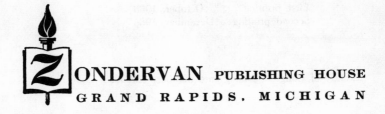

**Z**ONDERVAN PUBLISHING HOUSE
GRAND RAPIDS, MICHIGAN

Appreciation is expressed to the Billy Graham Evangelistic Association for the many photos of team members
supplied for this book.

First printing.......October, 1966
Second printing...December, 1966

Library of Congress catalog card number: 66-29033

# INTRODUCTION

In March, 1966, we participated in one of the most amazing evangelistic efforts we as a team have ever witnessed anywhere in the world.

It was amazing in its attendance. In 10 days nearly 300,000 people attended, a record for the size of the city.

It was amazing in that the crusade auditorium — Textile Hall — is one of the largest indoor arenas in the world. It is larger than Madison Square Garden in New York City!

It was amazing in that three cities fully cooperated with committees, choirs, counselors, ushers, etc.

It was amazing in the coverage given by the mass media. Television, daily newspapers, radio, weekly newspapers gave a wider and more intensive coverage than any city we have ever been to.

It was amazing in the united church support given over such a wide area. Only a handful of churches did not give complete support to the crusade. A few extreme fundamentalist and a few extreme liberal churches did not support it, but nearly all of the churches of all denominations gave the crusade all-out support.

It was amazing in that it was an interracial crusade in the deep South. Whites and Negroes sat side by side. The choir, ushers, counselors, committees, etc., were interracial. There was not one single unpleasant incident. As hundreds of people of both races came forward night after night, I watched them in thanksgiving to God that this was happening in the South. It was underscored once again that there is no color bar at the cross of Christ.

The crusade was amazing in its community support. The mayors, city councils, state governor, United States senators, and state legislature cooperated in every conceivable way. The police did a fantastic job in handling the traffic jams as thousands of cars converged on Textile Hall twice an evening.

The crusade is amazing in its continuing results. We are hearing stories constantly of people whose lives were changed during the crusade — who in turn are helping lead others to Christ.

The crusade was amazing in its leadership. Dr. L. D. Johnson, pastor of the First Baptist Church of Greenville, South Carolina; Dr. Wallace Fridy, pastor of St. John's Methodist Church, Anderson, South Carolina, and Dr. James S. Day, pastor of Calvary Baptist Church, Spartanburg, South Carolina, had on their committees the social, religious, political and racial leadership of the Southern Piedmont.

We believe that during March of 1966, heaven bent low in the Southern Piedmont. Our team sang with the committee and the ministers with a new fervor, "To God be the glory, great things He hath done."

One of the great contributing factors to the success of the crusade was the overwhelming support of *The Greenville News* and *Greenville Piedmont*. The editor of *The News*, Wayne Freeman, an Episcopal lay reader, served on the Crusade Executive Committee. If ever a newspaper went "all out," his did. We are grateful to the management of The Greenville News-Piedmont Company, especially J. Kelly Sisk and B. H. Peace, Jr., for giving the editors, reporters and photographers full support and extra space each day with which to work, in covering the crusade from every angle.

At the last Executive Committee meeting during the actual crusade, Mr. Freeman announced that Lewis Brabham, Sunday editor of *The Greenville News*, would write a book telling the story of the Southern Piedmont Crusade. Mr. Brabham went to work immediately — and the volume he has written, *A New Song in the South*, is the thrilling story! To the people who attended the Southern Piedmont Crusade or watched it on television from coast to coast, the book will bring back warm memories. To those who did not have an opportunity to attend or watch it, it will be a thrilling story of how God worked in a great Southern community. We believe this book will be an inspiration and challenge not only to the people of this generation, but to the generation to come.

BILLY GRAHAM

# PREFACE

Many articles and books have been written about Billy Graham, his life and his achievements, and these pages are not intended to review or duplicate other works. The story, in no wise a biography, presents the world-renowned evangelist only in the scope of the Southern Piedmont Crusade.

A learned scholar and theologian as well as a powerful preacher and personality with a deep concern for humanity, he is the holder of many degrees and special honors, but I chose to call him Billy throughout the book, instead of Doctor Graham. Wherever he goes he is a towering ambassador for Christ; everywhere he is a symbol of Christian evangelism, and around the world he is known as Billy Graham — also as just Billy.

Writing the story, as a newspaperman privileged to observe him and his dedicated team in action and to talk with individuals whose lives were touched by the Graham message, has been a regaling and inspiring experience for me.

This is an account of a memorable religious endeavor, a foray into Satan's territory, a high point in the history of an old, progressive city of the deep South, a campaign in which people were led into the light and knowledge of Almighty God.

No report, however voluminous, could embody all of the happenings of the 15-service crusade. No earthly being has the full record. And in a very real sense, there cannot be a final chapter since the drama for time to come will continue to unfold and develop in the hearts and lives of countless numbers.

To the many individuals and groups who have given help and guidance during the preparation of this report I wish to express indebtedness. I thank the management of the Greenville News-Piedmont Company for allowing me to write the book, to use pictures made by its photographers, and for cooperation in every way. I am especially grateful to Wayne W. Freeman, editor of *The News,* for his encouragement and aid from the start and for writing the foreword, and to *News* City Editor James Walker for his support and invaluable assistance.

Special thanks go to Dr. Cort Flint for obtaining a storehouse of material from many sources for use in the volume and for his contribution which is a part of Chapter 14.

I express gratitude to Billy and Ruth Graham for graciously receiving my wife and me at their home as information for the story was being compiled, and for his expressions in the introduction to the book.

I acknowledge indebtedness to members of the Graham organization for help and courtesies. Particularly I want to thank Cliff Barrows, Miss Bonnie Barrows and other members of the Barrows family; his secretary, Miss Jackie Edwards; John Lenning, Dr. T. W. Wilson, Dr. Grady Wilson, George M. Wilson, Willis Haymaker, Dr. Sherwood E. Wirt, Forrest Layman, Lee Fisher and Ray Harvey.

Dr. L. D. Johnson, crusade chairman; Dr. Wallace Fridy, Dr. James S. Day, Jr., and James B. Orders, co-chairmen; Dr. Gordon Blackwell, Dr. Thomas L. Neely, the Rev. William P. Palmer, B. O. Thomason, Jr., Max M. Rice and other steering committee members provided help and encouragement.

Deep appreciation goes to my wife, Evelyn, who assisted in many ways and typed the manuscript, without neglecting her role as mother of four school-age girls, and to Pat Zondervan and Floyd W. Thatcher, publishers, for their understanding and counsel during the preparation of the contents.

Lewis F. Brabham

Greenville, S. C.
August 10, 1966

# FOREWORD

In a personal letter written while the Southern Piedmont Crusade in Greenville was at its height, Billy Graham expressed a feeling of awe and fascination in the presence of newspapermen, due in part to "the tremendous power they wield" and in part to his frustrated desire to be one of them.

He should no longer feel uncomfortable, if that was the effect he was describing. There was a time when Billy was considerably "roughed up" by the press wherever he went. It was largely the result of the natural skepticism toward evangelists as a group. But we are convinced that the era of fundamental hostility began to end for Billy Graham in Greenville more than a year before he actually opened the crusade in March. He is now accepted and admired nationally by responsible newsmen.

Of course, he is going to encounter "hard-nosed" questions from reporters wherever he goes. Some will be hostile. Some will never accept him and — more important than the man and his career — his mission in the light that we came to see him as he pondered whether to conduct a crusade in his "homeland," as he made the decision and followed through.

The Southern Piedmont Crusade, we believe, added a new dimension to the ministry of this humble but powerfully compelling man. It was evangelism through journalism. Billy himself has told enough of the story of how our two newspapers, *The Greenville News* and the *Greenville Piedmont,* marshalled their full reportorial, editorial and technical forces to cover, as completely as any big story has ever been covered anywhere, that crusade.

We backed up our specialist in news of religion with two or more general reporters and a couple of capable volunteers. The police and City Hall reporter went to the crusade hall from scenes of violence and controversy. The court reporter finished his stint at the courthouse and joined him. Both were assigned to do "color" and "sidebar" stories and were inspired to produce "literature under pressure." Four photographers made hundreds of pictures.

Everyone who had a part "wrote over his head" and the two toughest reporters of the lot "went forward" before the ten days were finished. How all of the material got through the mechanical process, while editors, printers and deliverymen took all kinds of chances with delayed deadlines and presstime "hold," we probably never will know.

But the important thing was readership. Our staff filed on the Associated Press wires every line permitted by time and the flow of the news. Pictures went out electronically in batches. Sheer reader demand compelled every other newspaper in the region to follow our lead, and the national news wires carried full stories.

Was it worth it? Did it work? The answer is a resounding "YES!" Letters to the editor from people who weren't present said they felt they had been there after reading the full details. Letters from readers who attended said they relived the experience in the printed words.

Billy Graham should no longer stand in awe of the "fourth estate." He can handle the hard reportorial questions because he knows what he is saying and doing, and because he is one of us. He writes a widely read syndicated column — and he is traveling the world over reporting and commenting on the greatest story in all human history, the Gospel of Jesus Christ.

And what a reporter and interpreter of the Gospel he is!

On the morning the crusade began, we commented editorially, in part:

> But let people of all sorts and conditions come for whatever reason, even idle curiosity or to satisfy their preconceived notions of skepticism. They, together with the unknowing, the uncommitted, the committed by inactivity, the confused,

the doubting and even the agnostics and the avowed atheists, all of these, really are the ones for whom the Crusade is designed.

They are the ones among whom Billy Graham has found the greatest challenge for the Gospel he preaches.

Having been among the skeptics at the beginning of this man's evangelistic career more than a decade and a half ago, we think we can write of him objectively.

And we dare today's skeptics and the scoffers to expose themselves to what takes place in a vast audience when Billy Graham mounts the pulpit with the familiar Bible in his hand, or especially, when they meet him personally.

The criticisms one has heard of him and his methods soon will be forgotten under the thrust of his message, words of magnitude for their very humility, of impact for their undeviating directness. He preaches the simple, basic Christian gospel which is found with little variation in every pulpit in Greenville, nothing less nor more.

Billy Graham is no ordinary man, although he may resentfully deny that he is more than a willing instrument for the spreading of the Gospel. Personally, he is both simple and complex, warmly friendly yet detached, drawn to others yet affecting them as a magnet.

When he starts preaching, though, he seems to be transported, lifted out of himself and projecting something he dares not try to understand in its entirety, nor to attempt to explain by pragmatic logic alone.

Let those who would trap him beware. The simple but compelling preacher is a learned theologian. As one "high churchman" of our acquaintance said upon hearing him a year ago, while he considered coming here, "The rest of us have read and studied the great theologians of our time. But he has done that, and gone and questioned and listened to them, too."

This reporter-editor has been involved in one way or another in most of the big stories, national and state, of his and Billy Graham's time. But no political campaign, presidential or senatorial interview or government policy meeting has produced the drama of the crusade.

In the mid-Fifties, we were part of a group which met with Billy and decided the time was not yet. In 1965, we were convinced the time had come, and we now confess to Billy that, in part, he was the object of a carefully planned editorial campaign. On the day he met with a thousand or more clergymen and lay leaders, we wrote under the headline, "The Day of

Decision is Here!" We urged him to come and we followed it up with a pledge of support.

We served on the Executive Committee in which was vested local authority and responsibility. It turned out to be one of the most exciting experiences of our life. The planning had been done on a tri-county basis, and some of the committees were properly concerned about the pulling power of such a campaign in a busy era. We kept insisting that *The Greenville News* covered 10 to 15 counties and that news stories alone, without carefully conceived advertising, would draw heavily from that region of close to a million persons.

That is what happened. Billy opened to a capacity crowd on Friday night and on Sunday the overflow was half enough to fill the auditorium again. The crowd was unmanageable and the situation was obviously dangerous — both to the public and to the success of the crusade. On Monday a small group met with Billy Graham and Cliff Barrows to decide what to do. Billy's solution was double services, in the late afternoon and evening, which raised three major questions: could the police handle the outgoing and incoming traffic? could the evangelist stand the pace? when could it be started?

The police said they would try, and Billy said he could do it. It was suggested that the plan go into effect Thursday, to allow time to get the word out. We insisted on Tuesday, or Wednesday at the latest, on grounds that the region could be saturated with the information in 24 hours. Wednesday was the compromise date.

Logistically for the police and physically for Billy, the plan seemed impossible. We were certain only of the timing. But it worked. On Wednesday afternoon some 15,000 attended the first service; that night 20,000 were on hand. The taping of the television series started with the evening service, and Billy came on stronger than ever. Police licked their problem, asking only an additional 15-minute spread to move cars out of one end of the parking lots and the new crowd in the other.

It was one of those once-in-a-lifetime things. It couldn't have been done with mere human power, but it was done. And everyone concerned grew in knowledge, stature and strength. The work continues in Greenville and for thousands of square miles around. From our observation, it seemed that the Graham team gained new momentum in the face of adversity which carried them on to a new triumph in London three months later.

The next best thing to attending a crusade is to read about one. This is a newspaper-style book, crackling with facts, written against a close deadline and telling the great story of the Southern Piedmont Crusade as it unfolded.

The best thing of all, of course, is to participate in a crusade — so long as you don't try to keep up with Billy Graham's pace; it takes a team to do that. It is an experience that will never let go of your mind, heart and spirit.

WAYNE W. FREEMAN
Editor, *The Greenville News*

# Contents

Introduction

Preface

Foreword

1. Billy Graham's Only Crusade in America in 1966   19

2. The Fruits of the Crusade   26

3. Billy Graham's Arrival in Greenville   32

4. The Graham Home   36

5. The Spirit of America   42

6. Two Days Before the Opening   48

7. The Crusade Got Off to a Rainy Start   54

8. 'Jesus Demands Self-denial . . .'   62

9. Before Noon on Sunday   75

10. To a Well-known Anderson Clergyman   82

11. The Present Generation of Young People   94

12. The Billy Graham Evangelistic Association   102

13. During the Days of the Crusade   108

14. Billy Graham Came to Greenville   114

15. The General Assembly of South Carolina   127

16. The Southern Piedmont Crusade on Television   133

17. The Magnitude and Impact of a Billy Graham Crusade   140

18. Favorite Verses   150

19. Crusade Quotes   152

# A NEW SONG
## in the South

A recent photo of Dr. Graham (Courtesy Billy Graham Evangelistic Association)

One of the Greenville Crusade crowds (News-Piedmont photo)

# 1

BILLY GRAHAM'S ONLY CRUSADE IN AMERICA IN 1966 WAS CONducted in one of the South's fast-growing industrial centers, Greenville, South Carolina. In ten days 278,700 people — four and one-half times the population of the city proper — jammed into the crusade auditorium for the services.

The spirit and response, Evangelist Graham said, was "just like old-time revivals."

During the 15 services 7,311 went forward to profess Christ as their personal Saviour or to rededicate themselves to the glorification of the Lord and the Christian way of life. In addition, some 2,900 decisions were registered when "The Restless Ones," the Billy Graham film release, was shown in Greenville, Spartanburg and Anderson on the heels of the crusade services. Many others were led to the Lord through the crusade telecasts.

These are statistics. But no figures can represent the imponderable blessing and the full and lasting effect of the Southern Piedmont Crusade on the region. No gauge can measure transformation in lives, strength added to moral fibers, or the degree of peace found by empty-souled humans.

The crusade, planned for months like other Billy Graham crusades, opened on Friday night, March 4, with an estimated 19,400 people pouring into the crusade auditorium, Textile Hall. This complex is more normally a show place for textile machinery, equipment and supplies for the biennial Southern

Parking lot of Textile Hall (News-Piedmont photo)

Lines awaiting entry to the Hall (News-Piedmont photo)

Textile Exposition. Holding more people than Madison Square Garden, it is the largest auditorium between New York and Houston's Astrodome, and nothing like a capacity or near capacity audience had been expected for the first few services of the ten-day series. On Saturday, March 5, however, 21,500 people thronged the building, and an additional 3,500 stood outside as Dr. Graham left the platform to speak briefly to them before the opening of the service.

By Sunday, when every seat in the hall was taken and 6,000 who could not jam inside were turned away, the crusade team and Executive Committee members knew that something had to be done to accommodate the growing crowds. On Monday night Dr. L. D. Johnson, pastor of the First Baptist Church in Greenville and chairman of the Crusade Executive Committee, made the announcement that Dr. Graham had agreed to hold two services nightly for the last five days of the crusade. With obvious joy Dr. Johnson reported from the pulpit that the response to the crusade "has simply exceeded anything we had any reason to expect."

Billy, in a brief statement, expressed regret that so many had to be turned away because of lack of space and said the team gladly accepted the two-sermons-a-day recommendation of Dr. Johnson's committee. "I believe that within the next few days we will be able to see an historic spiritual impact that will have a far-reaching effect on the entire Southeastern part of our country," he said. "There are many indications that we are on the threshold of a great spiritual awakening in this crusade." Many would say later that his words proved to be prophetic.

It was the first time in America that twin services were scheduled at a Billy Graham Crusade, although it had been considered for the 1957 Madison Square Garden series in New York. As many as three services were held in one day during the 1954 London Crusade, but the London auditorium was smaller than Textile Hall and the evangelist was 12 years younger then.

The Greenville decision to hold double services, crusade planners reported rejoicingly, was a highly satisfactory one albeit the evangelist's strength was taxed heavily, traffic police were hard-pressed at times between services with bottlenecks of cars and buses, and longer hours were required of team mem-

bers, choir singers, ushers and all participating in the unprecedented campaign to win souls for God. Everything turned
out on a grander, greater style — a broader-sweeping crusade
for Christ.

At the end of each sermon, always a down-to-earth interpretation of the Bible, Billy calmly urged his listeners to go down
the aisle and make decisions for Christ, to say "yes" to the
Saviour. From all walks of life, white and Negro inquirers
came by the hundreds, quietly and reverently, when the invitation was given. No fewer than 214 went forward at any service,
and on Thursday night 1,300 responded to the altar call.

All over the world people prayed for the crusade. Many
in the Southern Piedmont area — which stretches across north-
west South Carolina, the foothills of North Carolina and dips
into northeast Georgia — reported praying as they had never
prayed before. God hears and answers prayer and many sinners
gave their lives to Christ. God's blessings were immeasurable.

The change in plans to hold two services a day in Textile
Hall meant sacrifice on the part of many — the greatest sacrifice
of all by Billy Graham. "He is almost literally laying his health
on the line and only the Divine Power he urges others to call
on can sustain him," Editor Wayne Freeman said in an editorial
in *The Greenville News* commenting on plans for the dual
services.

> Dr. Graham recently has been fighting an infection which is
> not serious, but is aggravating and debilitating. He is under
> orders from his doctor to take things as easy as nature permits.
> But he puts everything he has, and more, into his sermons.
> Now he has agreed to do this not once a day, but twice within
> a period of three or four hours. It is a self-imposed task that
> only a man who is an athlete (golf, hiking and weight work)
> in training, and who is totally inspired, could perform.

Preaching before multitudes is unlike delivering a sermon
to a church congregation of a few hundred, the evangelist had
found out years before. A superabundance of energy and oratori-
cal effort are needed, he knew from experience, to present the
Gospel effectively and hold the prolonged attention of vast
audiences such as those filling Textile Hall. For the last five
days of the crusade Billy preached the same sermon twice
nightly, the second with all of the fervency and conviction of

the first, the same penetrating delivery and dramatic gestures.

Had the crusade carried over beyond 10 days Billy might not have been able physically to preach twice on the same date. He almost fainted in the pulpit near the end of the first sermon on the last day in Textile Hall.

That he faltered momentarily was not detected by the audience as there was no noticeable break in his sermon. His voice, as strong on the closing day as in the earlier sermons of the crusade, carried the same conviction of a man of God bearing the answer to many problems plaguing troubled hearts. Of those close to him on and near the platform, most would never have known that he came near fainting had he not revealed later the temporary feeling he experienced. His recovery was immediate and he poured out the remainder of his message forcefully, in the Graham style most of the world knows.

Although he felt tired from the demands of five days of dual appearances, he gave the final message with matchless conviction, eloquently and as always curling a Bible in his left hand. He preached on "The Great Judgment Day," as he had done three hours earlier, and read the text from Acts 17:22-34, which describes the Apostle Paul's famous message at Mars Hill in Athens. At no time during the final service did faintness threaten; he had been given the strength to pour out another great message from the Bible to masses of people. His altar invitation following the sermon brought 423 inquirers who made commitments to Christ.

In the sermon Billy likened Paul to a "flaming torch — blazing his way up and down the Roman Empire preaching of Jesus Christ crucified and raised from the dead." Lucille B. Green, religion editor of *The Greenville News*, the following day wrote this about Billy Graham and his description of Paul:

> Many who have heard Dr. Graham in recent days thought the description translated into the present day could have described the man who stood before them (in Textile Hall).

Billy Graham in his study.

Dr. Kenneth Chafin, Professor of Evangelism at Southern Baptist Theological Seminary, Louisville, Kentucky; Dr. Graham; Dr. Duke McCall, President of the Seminary; and Dr. Cort Flint of Anderson, South Carolina, on the day the establishment of a Billy Graham Chair of Evangelism at the Seminary was announced. (News-Piedmont photo)

Dr. Graham in the pulpit
during the crusade
(News-Piedmont photo)

Willis Haymaker, left, Associate Crusade Director,
with Assistant Fire Chief Charlie Wilson, who was at
Textile Hall daily and insisted on full compliance
with fire regulations.

# 2

THE FRUITS OF THE CRUSADE BEGAN TO APPEAR ALMOST IMMEDI-
ately — in inquirers who said their lives were changed, their
faith renewed; in a new spirit evident in churches; in calm, joy,
and love permeating homes where there had been discord and
separation. There was increased awareness that the Christian
message is real and vital. It was as if the seeds sown by Billy
Graham's pleas for repentance and dedication to God had fallen
on fertile ground, with the prospect of a harvest of new religious
fervor.

Like a gale the crusade struck Greenville, and it picked up
momentum along the way as crowds overflowed the cavernous
hall. The effect of the event, tornado-like with benign winds,
were spread over hundreds of miles. No area could ever be
the same again after such a spiritual revival of people brought
closer to God.

Billy's unprecedented outpouring of energy in holding dual
services for five consecutive days did not exhaust him. The brief
feeling of faintness he felt in the pulpit during the first sermon on
the final day was his only one. The Crusade developed into the
largest ever held in the South; multitudes had heard the Word
of God preached and God's praises sung; commitments had been
made. There was no change in the spirit of humility that left
Billy awed by the throngs that came, but the experience of the
great crusade "among my people," in a community near the

Graham home, had stimulated him anew, in spirit and in body. "It was as if he had taken a tonic," commented Willis Haymaker, associate crusade director.

On the day following his last Greenville sermon Billy went to Charlotte, North Carolina, to address the Executive Club of the city that evening. Prior to the speech, he talked with newsmen about the zeal of the crusade, the vast crowds, the response of the people. "I never saw anything like it," he said. "It was the warmest response we've ever had. When we began turning away thousands at every service, there was nothing to do but go to two services a night." Strength to meet the challenge of the mushrooming crusade had been given to him by the Great Physician, reflected in his enthusiasm and buoyant spirit.

For a few weeks after the Greenville Crusade, he rested and worked at his mountain home and offices at Montreat, N. C., preparing for the mid-year crusade in London.

All that happened in the lives of the people who heard God's word preached during the ten momentous days of the Southern Piedmont Crusade can never be known, but some of the impact it made was noticeable almost immediately. "All over Greenville, Spartanburg and Anderson and the surrounding area," Editor Sherwood E. Wirt wrote in *Decision* magazine, "new shoots were springing up — good seed, growing in good soil, nourished by living water, giving promise of eternal fruit."

A 1966 court report completed during the summer following the crusade indicated a 25 per cent reduction in crime in Greenville County from 1965. The court solicitor attributed this in part to the crusade.

Judge J. Wilbur Hicks of the Greenville Juvenile and Domestic Relations Court reported two weeks after the final crusade service that an unusually large number of cases scheduled to come up before him for the days after the crusade closed were settled without the husbands and wives appearing. He credited some of this to the preaching of Billy Graham. "A considerable number of people have been calling my office to report that they have gotten together. The crusade so saturated the community that it is bound to have some good effects." He noted that families appearing before him during and soon after the crusade almost invariably made favorable mention of Graham and the services.

Relating an incident in which a woman had dropped charges of non-support against her husband, Probation Officer Horace H. McKown, Jr., of Greenville said the husband "made a decision for Christ at one of the Graham Crusade meetings and he and his wife are reuniting."

A well-known Greenville lawyer told of what had appeared to be another broken home in the making, until Billy Graham came to Greenville. Here are his words: "A wife who was filing for divorce came to my office with her husband. They told me that each of them had gone to the crusade on a different night and that as a result of Billy Graham's messages they were back together again."

Records of the Juvenile and Domestic Relations Court in Greenville indicate that family strife ordinarily reaches high tide in March, April and May. Not so, however, in the spring following the crusade. Judge Hicks said he thought it was a major factor in bringing about genuine relaxing of inter-family strife in many instances.

A young man and young woman who went forward and were counseled had no idea a few hours earlier of attending a religious meeting or of even visiting Greenville. They were hitch-hiking across the country after leaving college in a distant state.

A Greenville traveling salesman, one of the crusade counselors, found the couple "thumbing" on an interstate highway and gave them a ride. He talked of the crusade and offered to give them lodging for the night in his home if they wished to hear Billy Graham preach. Lukewarm to the idea, they accepted the invitation after some hesitation.

The girl, a tall blonde, was wearing jeans, boots and leather jacket. The young man might have been described as a beatnik type. They were guests of the salesman and his wife at the evening meal and accompanied them to Textile Hall for the service. When the appeal was given the two erstwhile college students were among the first to move down the aisle to the foot of the platform. Before the girl was halfway there a Christian matron slipped out of her seat and followed her. Another counselor, Bible in hand, moved behind the young man

All ages took enthusiastic part in the singing at crusade services (News-Piedmont photos)

to offer him aid. They blended into the crowd gathered quietly at the front, standing facing the speaker.

The girl said that she had been deeply stirred by the message and wanted to surrender her life to Christ. They were counseled at the service, and that night in the Greenville home, the salesman and his wife stayed up to counsel with them until early morning hours.

From Texas a man flew to bring a friend, a 78-year-old Greenville native, to the crusade. "I had to," the Texan said. "A Christian must be concerned about his friends. I had not been able to get Christ across to him. But Billy did, praise be to God!"

The aging former Greenvillian walked slowly to the altar and, standing with others, was heard to exclaim, "Praise be to God! I've found Jesus in time."

An eleven-year-old girl who came forward in life commitment was so solidly grounded by her counselor and advisor that she went home and led her father to Christ.

A Furman University professor who responded to the appeal said, "I found that I had to come as a little child." He was started on a Bible study program.

A college professor turned newspaper reporter interviewed the evangelist in his motel room and found himself suddenly in the throne-room of God, talking to his Saviour. Up to that time, he said, he had approached the Christian story strictly through the head with no heart. Billy assured him the story of salvation stands up under either, but God gave both heart and head to use for Him.

A church member for thirty years, a robust but graying man wept at the last service. "I was the one Billy talked to when he said many church members were exposed to just enough religion to let their souls go to hell," he said. "My name has been on the church books but I had never accepted Christ in my heart as my Saviour. Today I received the new birth."

Outside Textile Hall a policeman directing traffic told an usher he had been listening to the message. "Now I understand about eternity," he said.

On the opening night a man who had been separated from his wife was in the crusade audience. When the evangelist gave the invitation the man went forward to make a decision for Christ. His wife, singing in the choir, saw him come forward with others. Leaving her place she descended the steps and joined her husband in the circle of the committed, where they embraced.

Circuit Court Solicitor B. O. Thomason, Jr., who was sitting on the platform, noted what had happened. Later he remarked, "In the courtroom I see couples being separated; here we see couples being united."

# 3

BILLY GRAHAM'S ARRIVAL IN GREENVILLE, A BULWARK OF THE
Bible Belt and the "Textile Center of the World," came at a
time when the Piedmont region hungered for what he and his
organization had to offer. Planned originally as a tri-county
effort in Greenville, Spartanburg and Anderson, the crusade
expanded to embrace eventually a dozen or more counties.
Every home within a seventy-mile radius of Greenville was
visited between February 22 and February 28 and the residents
were invited to attend the crusade. Eight thousand men and
women took part in this widespread "threshold and visitation"
program, directed by a Greenville layman, Max McGee Rice,
and his twenty assistants.

Twenty thousand volunteers, counting the home visitors, the
3,200 choir members, 1,200 ushers, 1,300 counselors and advisors,
and the other workers and committee members, played roles in
making the crusade a success.

Organizing for the crusade was begun a year in advance,
so numerous were the details, so broad the scope, so diversified
the activity of the massive regional effort. The aim was to
bring the Gospel of Jesus Christ to the attention of as many
people as possible, to everyone in the Southern Piedmont section of the nation.

The counselors and advisors were trained intensively in
lecture study periods held in churches beginning in January

and ending on the eve of the crusade. At each service in Textile Hall they were assigned to counsel those who came forward in answer to the invitation.

Lovingly, quietly, skillfully they carried on the work for which they had been trained, always using a relaxed approach. Their service for the Master was rendered with such finesse that the audiences were scarcely aware that an extra measure of help was at each inquirer's shoulder.

There were 200 advisors, many of them ministers, and 1,100 counselors, all over sixteen years of age. They were prepared to counsel inquirers of similar age. Special counselors were appointed to work with children.

The chairman of the important counseling phase of the crusade was the Rev. Cullen Crook, pastor of Welcome Baptist Church in Greenville. The instructors were Forrest Layman, crusade director who also was in charge of the crusade office at 114 North Spring Street, and John Lenning, both members of the Graham organization.

Training sessions were held in Anderson, Spartanburg, Greer, Clinton and Pickens, as well as in Greenville. Special sessions were conducted at Toccoa Falls Bible Institute, Toccoa, Ga.; Columbia Bible College in the South Carolina capital, and Fruitland Baptist Bible Institute in Hendersonville, N. C.

On the night before the first crusade service Billy spoke at Textile Hall to the counselors and advisors, who had met for final briefing. He pointed out that the counselor concept goes back to Christ's fundamental method. "Let the priest and the evangelist concern himself with equipping the people. Equip the people of God, and let them do the work of Christ; thus can the ministry be multiplied."

The appearance of the evangelist was unscheduled and came as a joyous surprise. The meeting was a last day training session for ushers as well as counselors and was the first gathering of the huge crusade choir. Nearly 5,000 people, the majority of them choir volunteers, turned out in rainy weather for the briefing and rehearsal.

It was a homecoming for Cliff Barrows, beloved Greenville member of the Graham team, crusade music director and master of ceremonies extraordinary. The Barrows family has lived in Greenville since 1950.

The volunteer singers evidenced their training in quickly adjusting to Barrows' direction. Each section was asked to stand — sopranos, altos, tenors and basses. "Now, if you sing any other part," Cliff said with a smile known over most of the world, "we still welcome you."

"I don't remember an opening night rehearsal that thrilled me as much," he said after the choir under his leadership rehearsed a half dozen songs which included "There's a New Song in My Heart," "Just As I Am" and "Blessed Assurance."

The gathering applauded after Cliff presented Billy Graham as a "man with a message for our crusade whose personal life and whose messages have meant so much to our team."

The evangelist, mindful of the great burden of prayer which had gripped the Piedmont area with its more than 5,000 cottage prayer meetings held prior to the crusade, said that "thousands of men, women and young people are going to have an encounter with Jesus Christ that will make an impact in this community for years to come."

"We're not here to put on a show," he added. "We're here to magnify Jesus Christ and to present Christ as the answer to dilemmas we face."

The Billy Graham Crusade counseling and follow-up process is precise and definite. From the moment an individual accepts the evangelist's invitation to make a decision for Christ and comes forward, a trained counselor is assigned to him. The counselor (always of the same sex as the inquirer) with open Bible attempts to meet his needs by discussing his problem and committing the entire matter to God in prayer. A mature and experienced advisor then checks with the counselor to determine if the personal needs of the inquirer are met.

Within twenty-four hours the pastor of a church selected by the inquirer receives a copy of the inquirer's "decision card" with a letter requesting the pastor to meet with the person immediately. The pastor then returns a postage-paid card to the Crusade office indicating that he has contacted the inquirer and is attempting to bring him into the work and fellowship of the church.

The behind-the-scenes work of sorting the cards and mailing them to the pastors is handled by teams of volunteer follow-up workers. These may often work through the night in order to make the 24-hour deadline. Within forty-eight hours, a church representative visits each person who went forward. The chairman of the Greenville Follow-up Committee was James M. Fuller.

Another phase of the follow-up program involves Bible study courses. Inquirers are given Bible study sheets. When these are returned, a committee of volunteers grades them promptly and returns them to the inquirer along with another Bible study lesson. Max Greer was Bible study captain for the Greenville Crusade.

A series of letters goes to the inquirer from the crusade office to encourage him in his new life and urge him to apply these four rules to his Christian life: 1. Pray daily. 2. Read the Bible daily. 3. Give evidence of new faith to others. 4. Find a place in the work and fellowship of the local church.

At least one Greenville counselor had the opportunity to serve and witness for Christ prior to the crusade. Three nights before the first service at Textile Hall, Robert J. Edsall, a Greenville salesman, was staying at a motel in Atlanta, Ga. A man rapped at his door and asked if he owned the car parked out front bearing a Billy Graham Crusade sticker. Mr. Edsall replied that the car was his and that he was a counselor for the crusade beginning the following Friday in Greenville.

A friendship was formed with the visitor, a resident of Cincinnati, Ohio, revealing a problem that was troubling him. God can help, Mr. Edsall said, referring him to the Bible and words of Jesus.

"We prayed a little, then he prayed, and I prayed some more," the Greenville man related. "Then, in his own words, he made a commitment to Christ."

That weekend the Cincinnati man came to Greenville and attended three consecutive crusade services. At one of them he went forward to make a public profession of his newly found faith. On Sunday morning he accompanied the Edsall family to worship services at Aldersgate Methodist Church and heard a sermon by the pastor, the Rev. James W. Covington.

# 4

THE GRAHAM HOME IN THE MOUNTAINS NEAR MONTREAT, N. C.,
is about 80 miles from Greenville, as the crow flies. Billy told one
of his crusade audiences, "This is my home; these are my people."
When he decided to accept the invitation to lead the crusade
he wondered how he and the team would be received, recalling
the words of Jesus upon returning to His people: "A prophet
is not without honor, save in his own country, and in his own
house."

And so Billy, his humility unchanged, was gratified in an
unusual way that great numbers attended the services and that
thousands of his home people had made decisions for Christ.
"They do not come to hear me," he said. "They come to hear
the word of God. I am not a great teacher, or a great person.
I would be nothing without God."

Weeks before he came to Greenville a spiritual awakening
was beginning to be felt in widely separated parts of the Piedmont as hundreds of homes were opened for prayer for the
crusade.

"The Southern Piedmont must have the greatest concentration
of prayer this tri-state area has ever known," Billy said a month
before his first crusade sermon. "If we were not certain that
Christians would be praying for us, we would not dare attempt
this crusade."

The crusade opened with undergirding by 5,000 prayer groups that accounted for an estimated 675,000 man-hours of organized group prayer in Anderson, Spartanburg and Greenville areas — equivalent to 4,018 weeks or seventy-seven years of solid prayer. The Piedmont prayer groups were twice the number of prayer groups organized in the Boston area by the end of that great crusade.

"This is God's doing," said the veteran crusade organizer, Willis S. Haymaker. "It is glorious that so many people are praying for the crusade. It will be an immeasurable blessing to this part of the country."

Mostly women, but many men, gathered in small groups — twos, fives, twenties — in homes, offices, shops, schools to read prayer cards or speak from their own hearts. They tuned in on special fifteen-minute prayer-time radio programs broadcast daily Monday through Friday by three stations — WAIM in Anderson, WFBC in Greenville and WORD in Spartanburg. Billy Graham, Cliff Barrows and other team members were heard on the prayercasts.

"If the crusade meetings never started, the Piedmont area would realize great results through the prayer groups," Billy said at a news conference on the eve of the crusade. "The pastors tell me there is already a mobilized spirit of revival." Dr. C. Newman Faulconer, pastor of the Greenville First Presbyterian Church and general chairman of the Crusade Prayer Committee, expressed the belief that the local prayer groups would permanently strengthen the prayer life of the individuals and undergird the total program of local churches in a spirit and to an extent never known before.

In one new residential development, six housewives met for morning prayer services. All had moved to Greenville in recent months or years and each represented a different part of the country. Strangers at the outset, their accents differing, they prayed together and developed a fast and enduring Christian friendship.

Mrs. L. D. Johnson, wife of the crusade general chairman and First Baptist Church pastor, said her prayer group had brought the unique experience of praying intimately with members of other denominations — Presbyterians, Episcopalians, Methodists, Lutherans — in unity of spirit and purpose.

"So good to know your neighbors personally, and not just geographically!" exclaimed a matron, who admitted to nodding acquaintance only with those who had moved recently into the neighborhood.

A young bride shyly said she had actually avoided her neighbors because she felt they were snobbish. She realized she was wrong after being with them in prayer groups and confessed that part of the blame was hers for not meeting them at least halfway.

One woman who had been in deep mourning for a lost one came from her neighborhood prayer service with new strength and a brighter outlook.

Many housewives said they now were going about their daily chores in prayer for many things. A woman describing herself as a "worrier" experienced a new peace when she took her troubles to the Lord in prayer.

In more than one home the maid was called in from ironing and other work to add her prayers and join in the period of meditation. An adult Sunday school teacher told her class that she had put down the name of her yardman on the prayer card. "During the crusade he was converted," she said. "Prayers were answered."

Prayer leaders were selected by their pastors and organized nearly three months before the start of the crusade. Packets of material were assembled in the crusade office and distributed at prayer planning and instruction meetings held for leaders on Sunday afternoons in January.

Even as the crusade approached, the faith and dedication of thousands participating in the group prayer services had grown deeper. Many neighborhoods made plans to continue prayer groups on weekly or monthly schedules. The wife of a well-known attorney sparked this idea in her community. Richly blessed with material things, she now found something more satisfying and necessary in the communion of shared prayers.

The prayer movement was given impetus at a pre-crusade Prayer Rally held at Pendleton Street Baptist Church in Greenville on Sunday afternoon, February 6. The guest speaker was Mrs. Fred Dienert of Philadelphia, Pa., an active member in the Business and Professional Women of America and a national advisor for Christian Women's Club. The rally, attended by about 1,000, served as a focal point for the home and business prayer meetings and initiated the "Prayer-Time" radio broadcast.

In an evangelistic message Mrs. Dienert sounded the call for conversion, urging those at the rally to "become fingers of God," strengthened by His touch, so that they might reach out and in turn convert the unbelievers in their midst.

Willis Haymaker quoted the text of all Graham crusades: "If my people which are called by my name, shall humble themselves and pray, and seek my face, and turn from their wicked ways; then will I hear from heaven, and will forgive their sin, and will heal their land." (II Chronicles 7:14).

Dr. Faulconer, the crusade prayer chairman, said, "Prayer has surrounded this meeting since its birth." He added that the Greenville Ministerial Association as well as lay groups had prayed two years for the reality of such a meeting in Greenville.

Billy felt certain that he had made the right decision when he accepted the invitation to lead the Southern Piedmont Crusade. "Ever since the decision I have had the feeling that God directed me here and I have had real peace of mind about it," he said.

Why did he choose this Southern textile city of 66,188 (1960 census) when he turns down hundreds of invitations every year, most of them from larger metropolitan areas?

For one thing, he faced a month-long crusade in London, England — from June 1 to July 2 — plus affiliated speaking engagements at Cambridge, Oxford and other universities, and numerous press conferences. All this would constitute a tremendous physical drain on him. Later in the year he would go to Poland and Germany for crusades and then participate in the World Congress on Evangelism, of which he is co-chairman, in Kongresshal in Berlin from October 26 to November 4.

Then, any crusade in the United States in 1966 had to be indoors because of the season. "The fine facilities of Textile Hall, the population potential were big factors," Billy said, "but even more is the fact that Greenville is the home of Cliff Barrows. When it comes right down to the final decision, however, I think probably the most important factor was the thousands of prayers that have been offered to make the Southern Piedmont Crusade a reality."

Dr. Graham made honorary citizen of Greenville by
Mayor David G. Traxler, right (News-Piedmont
photo); Below: Billy Graham Evangelistic Association
Board of Directors at 1965 meeting in Montreat,
North Carolina.

The negotiations and planning that led to the crusade had been going on over a period of nearly two years. There was an earlier massive effort made to bring the evangelist to Greenville. In September, 1957, Billy came to the city and spent a few hours with religious and civic leaders discussing the possibility of a crusade. But after a "lot of prayer and consideration" it was finally decided that the time was not right.

Down through the intervening years the Christian Business Men's Association continued to keep the idea alive. In 1964 a more concentrated effort was initiated and this brought Billy to Greenville March 26, 1965 to a prayer breakfast in Textile Hall attended by 1,450 Southern Piedmont ministers and laymen, indicating their support of the formal request made at the time.

Dr. L. D. Johnson, as chairman of the local group, extended the official invitation, and Billy said that while he would not give a definite answer at the time, the answer would probably be favorable. "I love this part of the country and Cliff Barrows has long wanted us to come here," he said. "If we come here we will come on our knees . . . and we will preach the Gospel of Jesus Christ and Him crucified." Several weeks later he wrote Dr. Johnson, accepting the invitation.

James B. Orders, president of the Orders Mattress Co. and co-chairman of the Southern Piedmont Crusade, served in 1963 and again in 1964 as president of the Christian Business Men's Association, which continued efforts over a long period to bring the Graham team to the city. "I wasn't among the first to work toward this end," Mr. Orders said, "but I caught the vision and kept up activity in this work."

# 5

THE SPIRIT OF AMERICA IS EXEMPLIFIED IN THE PIEDMONT OF the Carolinas, a vast workshop producing a variety and ever-greater quantities of goods for the nation and the world, an area of scores of colleges and universities, inhabited by self-reliant, determined, progressive people.

The industrial, business and residential growth of Greenville, Spartanburg and Anderson in recent years has been spectacular. Few cities of similar size have matched the strides, the bold "let's go" spirit found here. More than $100,000,000 of new industrial construction was announced in Spartanburg in 1965. Anderson is growing at an accelerated pace with one of its companies starting a $10,000,000 plant. Greenville counted $175,000,000 in new and major expansions of industry in the 1960-65 period.

This is the hub of the nation's largest textile manufacturing region, but recent years have seen the introduction of many other types of industries, providing a broader economic diversity.

Before the end of this century the Piedmont Crescent along the Carolina foothills and reaching into Georgia and Virginia may well become a single, continuous city. This development, indeed, already has more than commenced. Estimates placed Greenville County's 1966 population at 250,000 with over one million people living within a 100-mile radius of the city. It is 60 miles from Anderson to Spartanburg, and Greenville lies about midway between the two. All are connected by an interstate highway and other routes. Greenville and Spartanburg have a joint airport built in 1963 at a cost of $11 million.

Before World War II the three were small cities, or large towns by some standards. In 1966 they were burgeoning into one of the South's most dynamic and progressive areas, with full employment and affluence. Agriculture plays an important role in its economy, though to a lesser degree since the winds of new industrialization began howling.

The area's roots are deep in historic lore and the traditions of the old South, and it throbs with manufacturing and commercial activity. Yet it has been free of the racial strife that has torn and scarred other cities and sections of the nation. In the great crusade in Textile Hall, whites and Negroes worshiped together and sang side by side in the choir. There was integrated counseling. Two Negro crusade singers, internationally-known Ethel Waters and rising young star Myrtle Hall, received ovations when they appeared. "There's a new song in the new South," commented Cliff Barrows, paraphrasing the title of the popular melody of many crusade choirs, "There's a New Song in My Heart."

Nearly 70 per cent of the residents of Greenville County are church members, a 1964 interdenominational census indicated. Of 101,946 people included in the survey, 68,464 reported being members of a church. All except 9,219 said they attended church services at least once a month.

In the county some 500 churches represent about twenty-six different faiths. The churches are predominantly Baptist. In the city of Greenville 61 of its 126 churches are Baptist. The 1960 decennial federal census reported that of the 209,772 people living in Greenville County, about 100,000 claimed to be Baptists.

Mrs. Loulie Latimer Owens, special collections librarian at Furman University, tells of a brief conversation a Lutheran clergyman had with a Methodist pastor following the 1964 interdenominational census.

"Well, what did you learn from the census?" the Methodist asked.

"That I'm surrounded by Baptists," wailed the Lutheran.

The Billy Graham Crusade was, however, far from being an all-Baptist revival. It was truly an interdenominational undertaking with people of many religions making up the audiences. Representatives of eight different Protestant denominations composed the Crusade Executive Committee.[1] (See following page.)

[1]The following made up the Executive Committee: From Greenville — Dr. R. C. Blackwell, Furman University Mathematics Professor (Baptist); Nathaniel J. Brockman, Director of Baptist Education Center of Greenville (Baptist); Alfred F. Burgess, Attorney (Episcopal); Rev. Cullen Crook, minister (Baptist); Dr. J. Guy Douglas, Dentist (Baptist); Dr. Robert N. Dubose, Minister (Methodist); Dr. Morton T. Edwards, Dentist (Presbyterian); Dr. C. Newman Faulconer, Minister (Presbyterian); Rev. David C. Francis, Minister (Baptist); Wayne W. Freeman, Editor (Episcopal); Rev. S. R. Glenn, Methodist District Superintendent; Thomas S. Hartness, Owner of Pepsi Cola Bottling Co. (Baptist); Rev. C. R. Hickman, Minister (Greenville); Phillips Hungerford, Banker (Episcopal); Rev. Clyde L. Ireland, Rector (Episcopal); Dr. L. D. Johnson, Minister (Baptist); Arthur Magill, Manufacturing company executive (Presbyterian); Rev. William W. McNeil, Minister (Methodist); James B. Orders, Jr., manufacturing company executive (Methodist); Rex O'Steen, President of Chevrolet agency (Presbyterian); Rev. William L. Palmer, minister (Baptist); DuPre Rhame, Furman University faculty member (Baptist); Max M. Rice, owner of mountain lodge (Baptist); Harrison Rearden, insurance executive (Baptist); Jack E. Shaw, construction contractor (Pentecostal); Rev. James T. Shealy, minister (Church of God); Col. C. E. Singleton, retired (Baptist); Dr. Bernard L. Trexler, Minister (Lutheran); B. O. Thomason, Jr., Court Solicitor (Methodist); Sidney M. Wilson, realtor (Baptist); James H. Woodside, insurance executive (Presbyterian); Murry Woodward, (Baptist).

Spartanburg — Lt. Col. Robert Amos (Methodist); Dr. William L. Ball, Jr., Minister (Baptist); Z. V. Beck, Jr., (Baptist); Evans Cannon, YMCA secretary; Jack R. Cannon (Methodist); Dr. James S. Day, Jr., minister (Baptist); O. H. Green (Methodist); Neville Holcombe, attorney (Episcopal); Rev. Coolidge Johnson, minister (Baptist); Rev. Everette L. Lineberger, minister (Lutheran); Dr. Fred Poag, minister (Presbyterian); Dr. John W. Robison, minister (Methodist); Dr. Capers Satterlee, clergyman (Episcopal).

Anderson — John Clark, manager of Sears store (Episcopal); Dr. Cort R. Flint, minister (Baptist); Dr. Wallace Fridy, minister (Methodist); Robert L. Hale, textile executive (Methodist); J. Roy Martin, Jr., roofing firm president (Baptist); Rev. James O. Rich, minister (Baptist); Dr. Morris Young, physician (Presbyterian).

Also, H. Preston Griffin, furniture company executive (Baptist) of Greer; Willis Haymaker, crusade associate, Lenoir, N. C.; K. W. Johnston (Wesleyan Methodist) of Greer; Rev. R. Von King, minister (Baptist) of Lyman; Forrest Layman, crusade director, Atlanta, Ga.; Roy McCall, Jr., manufacturing company president (Baptist) of Easley; Dr. T. L. Neely, president of North Greenville Junior College (Baptist) of Tigerville, S. C.; J. Harlon Riggins, accountant, Simpsonville; Stewart B. Simms (Baptist) of Greer; C. D. Williams of Mauldin, S. C.

Against the backdrop of diligent, cultural, church-going people in a thriving community, one might wonder why Greenville County felt the need for years for a crusade and never gave up its goal of bringing it about.

For one thing the continuing movement showed that many people were still interested in being Christians. Men knew that churches could gain new strength and that stronger churches would bolster the moral fiber of the community. Individuals' faiths needed to be deepened, threadbare religion reinforced. Lawlessness could be lessened and spiritual cowardice conceivably could be obliterated.

The crime rate in the area has been very much like the national pattern, except that there has been no known organized murder gangs and racketeers such as have plagued some metropolitan sections. As the population has grown the work load of law enforcement agencies and the courts multiplied. A number of crimes, including breaking and entering, stealing, assault and battery, have risen sharply in recent years. Upstate South Carolina authorities have been concerned over the increasing percentage of juvenile crimes. More than half of the defendants who appeared in General Sessions Court in Greenville in 1965 were between the ages of sixteen and twenty-three.

In order to reach as many people as possible, "Operation Andrew" was put into effect by the churches. Many Greenville area pastors say the plan did reach many unchurched and spiritual needy people in the southern Piedmont.

Operation Andrew was first conceived by a minister in London during the 1954 Graham Crusade and has been used in every crusade since. It takes its name from John 1:40 - 42: "Andrew . . . first findeth his own brother Simon . . . and brought him to Jesus."

Preparation was begun at initial meetings of prayer groups. Leaders explained that the purpose was to bring the unconverted and unchurched to crusade services by enlisting Christians as active "Andrews." Many who would not come to an ordinary service, it was pointed out, would attend evangelistic crusades if personally invited.

In the unique operation, individuals, Sunday school classes and other groups agree to attend the services, with each Christian bringing at least one other person who needs Christ. There are five steps in Operation Andrew: (1) Begin to pray for from one to ten people who have a spiritual need; (2) cultivate their friendship; (3) bring them to the services; (4) encourage them in Christian commitment; (5) follow them up until they are linked with the church and become growing, witnessing Christians. Each Christian in the group is asked to list the names of those for whom he wishes to pray on the back of a card and to carry the card in his Bible or study materials as a daily reminder.

Churches participate in Operation Andrew by group reservation. Textile Hall reservations were made for groups of 20 or more, with the understanding that half the reservations would be used by church members and the other half by unchurched people who would be brought to the crusade by the church members — often in chartered buses.

Hundreds who enlisted as active "Andrews" found themselves to be keener, more radiant witnesses for Christ. And many who reached the crusade through invitation from "Andrews" found Christ — and were also able to find satisfactory church homes.

The Southern Piedmont Crusade was planned carefully and in detail. Billy had been able to spend a number of weeks at Montreat and had given much thought and study to the messages he would bring to Greenville. He would lead a crusade in the section of the country in which he had grown up and in which he and his family now lived — an area he knew well.

The emphasis of his preaching, he decided, would be a little different than it had been in other areas. "I shall certainly preach sin and judgment," he said, "but the main thrust will be the love of God in Christ, reconciling the world unto Himself. Paul said to the Corinthians: 'I am determined to know nothing among you, save Jesus and Him crucified.' Therefore, the cross will be central in my preaching. The Gospel is both vertical and horizontal. The vertical has to do with our relationship to God. Jesus said, 'Thou shalt love the Lord thy God with all thy heart, mind, and soul.' The horizontal has to do with our relationship to our fellow man. Jesus also said, 'Thou shalt love thy neighbor as thyself.' Therefore the message of sin, judgment, and redemption will be accompanied by an emphasis on personal morality, ethical concepts and social justice."

Billy came to Greenville from Atlanta on the morning of Tuesday, March 1, and took advantage of the warm sunshine for a round of golf before beginning activities connected with the crusade. He and three others teed off at Green Valley Country Club shortly before noon. In the foursome were Bishop Paul Hardin, Jr. of Columbia, head of the Methodist Church in South Carolina; the Rev. Thomas H. Carson, Jr., rector of Christ Episcopal Church in Greenville, and B. Frank Mayfield, Greenville businessman. A gallery of half a dozen men followed the golfers.

After spending the best part of the day on the golf course and lunching with the party at the club, the evangelist found himself behind Bishop Hardin. The bishop shot a par 72 while Billy had an 88.

Billy faced a rather busy three-day schedule of speeches and conferences in Greenville prior to the first crusade sermon Friday night. The need to conserve his energy and build his strength is always present, and his exercises to achieve this need include hiking, running, weight-lifting and golfing.

Jim Anderson, sports editor of *The Greenville News*, wrote a piece about Billy's golf in which he included these two paragraphs:

> Dr. Graham was once asked, after a round here: "Dr. Graham, for a man who has accomplished so much, and is so gifted, why is it your golf game is filled with hooks and slices?"
>
> The reply of the world-famous evangelist was: "In everything else I do, I call on the Lord's help for guidance. In golf I go it strictly on my own."

Billy actually plays well for the short time he has for golf, which Editor Anderson explained, adding, "Dr. Graham could probably be a low handicap golfer if he could put more time to the game."

One morning during the crusade Billy enjoyed a round of golf with B. H. Peace, Jr., vice president of The Greenville News-Piedmont Co.

"God saved my soul; golf saved my body," Mr. Peace quoted the evangelist as saying.

# 6

TWO DAYS BEFORE THE OPENING OF THE CRUSADE IN TEXTILE HALL
Billy made his first Greenville public appearance, speaking to
the student body of Furman University. Furman, transplanted
from the heart of the city ten years ago to a 1,200-acre campus
with magnificent buildings and fountains almost in the shadow
of Paris Mountain, is one of Greenville's three religious colleges.

The address of the evangelist before 2,200 students and
others in McAlister Auditorium was carried live throughout the
Southern Piedmont by WFBC-TV, Greenville, and was beamed
at students in the area as an answer to their problems. Present-
ing him to the audience, Furman President Dr. Gordon W. Blackwell said, "Dr. Graham is one of America's dynamic voices and
has preached to more people than any man alive."

The evangelist then delivered a 40-minute speech in which
he listed many of the problems plaguing the student of 1966.
The mood of the student he pictured as that of the young man
who said to a speaker, "We want to demonstrate, but we need
a cause." Billy said he was convinced that cause is Christ.
"I want to present a case for Christ, for God and the Bible,"
he added.

Youth is becoming involved in all the world's social problems
because we are living in a world of crises, he continued. He
listed some of the problems challenging students: the war in
Viet Nam, political revolutions around the world, the sexual

48

energy question which he said was greater than the civil rights crisis, the population explosion, the technological crises, with scientific knowledge expected to double in the next 19 years — and the problem of human nature.

"Human nature! That is our greatest problem," Billy told them. "As long as one man hates there is danger of war. We can solve all of our other problems, but this one defies us."

The majority of those who attend his crusades are below the age of 25, he said. "They are looking for answers that aren't found in the classrooms."

Television cameras and all eyes of the Furman audience on him, Billy raised his Bible aloft and cried, "There is no answer to the world's dilemmas — or to your problems — save in this book. It is not a book of science . . . it is a book of redemption . . . it is the story of man's rebellion against God, and of God's redemption of man."

"God sent us His Son to tell us He loved us still . . . And because Christ died God forgave us. Only this forgiveness can release the guilt complex that tortures so many students. Christ is a reason for life and I come to this belief by faith."

Several students reported they were profoundly moved by Billy's message. A student at Clemson University, 40 miles west of Greenville, who read of the crusade and heard the broadcast, found God without attending a service.

> Mr. Graham, he wrote, you have won me for God, I just want to tell you how much your crusade is meaning to this part of the country.
>
> Yesterday I walked out of the dorm and walked to Lake Hartwell, away from everyone. I watched muskrats swimming, fish jumping, birds flying, and heard frogs. I walked on the mud and through the trees and briars. When I was at the Lake it was like reaching a major goal in my life. Then I got down on my knees and prayed to God to forgive me of my sins and to help me live my life for His sake.
>
> This prayer was, I guess, the most serious prayer that I ever made. I don't know how long I kneeled there but when I opened my eyes it was dark. I felt nearer to God than I ever had before. I walked back to the dorm feeling very happy and knowing that I was going to try to live for God more than ever. I know that I'll live a much better life now that I have accepted God . . . I never knew how great the glory of God was. You

have won me for God. Thank you for just being in this area.
Most of all thank God for your being able to help others who
haven't accepted God.

Even before the crusade began its benefits were beginning
to be felt. Forrest Layman was highly encouraged by the mount-
ing spiritual fervor and expectancy as the crusade neared.

The Billy Graham team set up headquarters at Holiday Inn
Motel at Pleasantburg Shopping Center, about a mile from Textile Hall. On Wednesday afternoon, two days before the crusade
opening, Billy told reporters at a news conference at the motel
that "even if the Southern Piedmont Crusade were to be can-
celled out today, this area would have achieved permanent
benefit. I have had pastors tell me already that their churches
are in a spirit of revival and spiritual renewal brought about
by the emphasis on prayer in preparation for the crusade. The
closeness, the interaction between denominations, the involvement of neighbors drawn close together in communion of prayer
groups . . . all of these will have lasting effect."

A newsman asked if commitments and professions of faith
at a crusade were lasting. Replying, Billy said the effort would
be worthwhile if only one soul was won for Christ. But it
takes five years or longer to begin evaluating the results of a
crusade. He cited the experience in Sydney, Australia, where
five years after the crusade churches were questioned. One
minister pointed to members then on his official board and on
the board of trustees who had come into the church through
commitments made at the crusade sessions. Perhaps half of his
church membership, he said, could be traced to the impact of
the crusade five years earlier.

"You really have to wait to evaluate the impact on the personal level, too," Billy added. "When an individual makes the
decision to accept Christ, and you ask him about it, he hardly
knows what has happened. But when you ask him five years
later, he can tell you of a changed life because of that decision."

Billy announced that he had received messages from a number of officials planning to attend the Southern Piedmont Crusade. Governor and Mrs. Robert E. McNair would join him
when the crusade opened Friday night in Textile Hall. U. S.
Senator and Mrs. Donald S. Russell would attend on Saturday

The evangelist and Governor
Robert E. McNair (left)

The empty auditorium (photo by Joe Jordan)

night, and U. S. Senator Strom Thurmond would attend the Sunday afternoon service.

The evangelist said he thought the Southern Piedmont Crusade would show the nation a spiritual unity and would witness what God is doing in the South.

Dr. L. D. Johnson interjected a comment that he said had been made to him by Yancey S. Gilkerson, executive vice-president of Textile Hall Corporation, while volunteers were setting up the more than twenty thousand chairs in the big Crusade auditorium. "This is the kind of ecumenicity in which I believe," Mr. Gilkerson said. "When you can see men of every Protestant faith, from churches across the city, Negroes and whites working side by side, sharing coffee breaks and conversation, this is ecumenical progress."

Announcement was made that the crusade had a budget of $161,000, to be filled by contributions, and that about $92,000 of that had been raised two days prior to the opening service.

In response to a question about what happens to Crusade converts, and follow-up procedure, the evangelist gave this answer:

"We never call them 'converts.' We much prefer to call them 'inquirers.' Only God knows when or if a man is truly converted. Many come forward in our meetings who are seekers but not finders. We have abundant evidence that the majority of those who respond to the invitation lead a transformed life from that moment on, but there are hundreds during the course of a crusade who are in various stages of spiritual development. Some even come forward out of curiosity, or perhaps because a friend has come, and they want to accompany them; therefore it would be presumptuous for us to call them 'converts.'

"Naturally, it is impossible for us to control what happens to any inquirer. If the Book of Acts really teaches us anything, it teaches us that the Holy Spirit is the great follow-up agent. In addition to encouraging the inquirer to become active in a local church, we have an extensive follow-up program. The inquirer is contacted a number of times, sent various types of Christian literature, and encouraged in many ways to grow in his spiritual knowledge of God."

The tone for the crusade was sounded the day before it started at a meeting of 650 ministers and Christian workers at Greenville's First Baptist Church. The major thrust would be the rededication of Christians, the evangelist said, explaining that the total number of outsiders saved would be relatively small "because almost everybody here claims to be affiliated with some church somewhere."

Billy predicted that many young people would dedicate themselves to Christian service. He added that Christian workers are greatly needed because not enough people are going to seminaries.

He also urged a united front in the crusade. "There is enough we can agree with," he said, even though "we are divided denominationally, theologically, racially, culturally, economically — and in the very seminaries we went to." He emphasized the need for spiritual preaching, prayer, witnessing and continuing evangelism.

Before the closing prayer was offered by Dr. C. Newman Faulconer, Billy asked those who would join him in rededicating themselves before the crusade to raise their hands. Nearly all present responded with uplifted hands.

"It now rests in God's hands what will happen and how He will use the preparations which have been made," commented Dr. Wallace Fridy of Anderson, crusade co-chairman, after the meeting. "Surely the churches which put the most in it will reap the greatest benefit. The real test will come in the years ahead."

# 7

THE CRUSADE GOT OFF TO A RAINY START. FOR MORE THAN TWO hours before the opening service, showers drenched the city and slowed traffic to a crawl. A bus-car collision at an intersection on Pleasantburg Drive, Textile Hall's main traffic artery, added to the vehicular congestion. It took 45 minutes for the two-mile drive from my home to the hall.

For Charles W. Scales, Jr., chairman of the crusade traffic committee, the night brought a full-scale preview of traffic and parking problems. Fifteen state highway patrolmen and several sheriff's deputies assisted city police, under Traffic Lt. Festus Hawkins, in directing crusade traffic. The 5,000 parking spaces included 2,500 on Textile Hall property and others granted by a number of commercial and private property owners adjacent to Pleasantburg Drive. Nearly all were used on the first night and no event in Greenville, except for a Christmas parade, had drawn so large a crowd, police reported.

Through the many doors of the huge concrete building a steady flow of people streamed, assisted by a team of ushers who had received instructions in their duties from Col. Clifford E. Singleton, Usher Committee chairman, at a meeting two nights earlier. For a time it appeared the hall would not hold the first-night crowd.

Billy, feeling "much better" after having been threatened by a slight cold earlier in the week, spent most of the day studying and preparing for the crusade. He was escorted in a police car from the Holiday Inn Motel to Textile Hall by Lt. Hawkins, who drove him to and from each service.

Cliff Barrows lifted his arms and 3,200 voices were raised in song to the glory of God. There was no doubt of the impact of a Billy Graham Crusade. Delighted, Cliff said he believed the "greater than expected" choir response was a foretaste of what God was going to do. He had anticipated a choir of 2,500.

This was an unaccustomed role for the big exposition complex, built to show off machinery and wares of the textile industry, reverberating now with the sound of voices blended in hymns of praise. In a mighty crescendo, the choir was singing "There's a New Song in My Heart" when the evangelist walked up the stairs and onto the platform. Only the few who happened to be glancing at the right place at the right time saw him. He was joined shortly by Governor Robert E. McNair, Greenville Mayor David G. Traxler, State Senator P. Bradley Morrah, Jr., and others.

Governor McNair spoke briefly and welcomed Billy to the state. "He's our neighbor," he said, "and is held in warm affection around the world." Later the evangelist replied, "I am not just a neighbor; we're kinfolks." His paternal grandfather, a Confederate veteran, moved to North Carolina from York county, South Carolina.

When Cliff stepped to the microphone and asked for a period of silent prayer, a stillness fell over the throng from the balcony to the choir loft and all one could hear was the hum of fans and motors and the very faint cry of one child.

"God be praised — this is one great night," Crusade Chairman Johnson said, viewing the vast audience estimated at 19,400 by Textile Hall officials. Like others, he had not expected to see Textile Hall so nearly filled the first night.

Before Billy Graham stepped up to preach, George Beverly Shea, baritone soloist and a member of the Graham team since 1947, sang "I'd Rather Have Jesus."

On the rostrum, the evangelist seemed overjoyed at the size of the crowd — one of the largest he had ever preached to on an opening night, he said. His probing eyes looked out over the audience from one end of the building to the other, before he began to speak.

Songleader Cliff Barrows in action (News-Piedmont photo)

"I believe nobody is here by accident. I believe it is the sovereignty of God that has made this possible. Among these thousands are many who have spiritual needs, problems you can't solve and sins that need forgiveness . . . and tonight many of you are going to have those spiritual needs filled, those problems solved, those sins forgiven."

His topic was "What It Means to Be a Christian in 1966." The text was Matthew 16:24: "Then said Jesus unto his disciples, If any man will come after me let him deny himself, and take up his cross, and follow me."

The world needs the guidelines of the Word of God, the Bible as never before, Billy said. "I would rather be alive at this moment of history than any other period. This is a challenging, thrilling and exhilarating hour to proclaim the Gospel of Jesus Christ . . . We are living in a time when American life is changing rapidly. The moral standards of yesterday are questioned and rejected. Corrupt practices are becoming the norm of behavior — cheating in school, lying in business and using sex to sell products . . . In the midst of our society Christianity is offered to men as an alternative to secularism and moral corruption.

"But thousands of people in the church are not Christians by the New Testament definition and standard. A Christian is a person who has the conviction that God is, that he has sinned against God, that Jesus Christ is the Son of God and that Christ can save him.

"Second, a Christian is a person who has made a commitment. It is a commitment to Jesus Christ without reservation. Faith involves the intellect, the emotion and the will . . .

"Third and finally, a Christian is a person who conducts himself like a Christian. We are told we must compromise and adapt a Christian way of life to fit in with the imperfections of a sinful world, yet God is calling us to be Christlike in the midst of a pagan, secular, immoral and difficult world."

At the end of the sermon Billy Graham urged the people to make a public commitment to Christ. "I'm going to ask you to get up out of your seats — hundreds of you — and come and stand here," he said, indicating the large area without seats in front of the platform. "You will want to lose your life to find a new life before God . . . while we bow our heads in prayer, come . . . ."

Don Hustad at the console organ and Tedd Smith at the piano began playing softly the strains of "Just as I Am, Without One Plea," and the choir joined in humming.

From seats throughout the building inquirers streamed to the front, adults and young people. "We will give you a packet of Scripture and Bible study verses," the evangelist explained. "You will have a prayer and go back to your seats. Your friends or family or bus will wait for you."

As he talked they continued to come, forming a semi-circle around the pulpit. Counselors with faces aglow and smiles of welcome stepped beside them to help. Overhead was a huge Biblical quotation painted on a yard-wide ribbon of starched sheeting: "I am the way, the truth and the life (John 14:6)."

"You have not come to me. You have come tonight to Jesus Christ, who can forgive you of your sins and change your life," Billy told the inquirer. A counselor would give each a packet, he said, that would explain the decision they had made. It would be good for them to get to the Scriptures immediately. "You may not know what you are reading at first, but God will speak to you," he said, advising the inquirers to "get to praying."

Two hundred and fourteen responded to the invitation, going forward to surrender or rededicate their lives as the first fruit of the harvest of the ten-day crusade. The first-night audience included about 500 Negroes and some of them were in the group who gave their hearts to Jesus.

One of the first to reach Textile Hall for the opening service was 82-year-old Mrs. Pearl Goode of Pasadena, Calif., who traveled alone across the country to attend the crusade. Three hours before the Graham message was delivered, Mrs. Goode arrived by taxi cab from her hotel and walked alone into the big hall. Her thoughts, she said, were concentrated on Billy and after looking over the auditorium, with its row after row of new folding chairs, she proceeded to the prayer room to offer prayers for him, just as she had done many times before in other places. This was the 36th Billy Graham crusade she had attended.

Every Sunday afternoon for ten years, from 1939 to 1949, Mrs. Goode drove thirty miles from Pasadena and back to see and hear Dr. Charles Fuller and his family broadcast on radio. Mrs. Goode, a nurse, had never heard of Billy Graham, but one night in 1949 she went to a big tent meeting in Los Angeles where he was preaching. She went back the next night and the next.

During the seventeen years following she had heard the tall North Carolina evangelist preach more than 500 times in crusades from New York to Honolulu.

She related to Gil Rowland, editor of religion of the Greenville *Piedmont,* that she became so ill in the 1950's that she asked God to "take me home." A widow, she continued to live nevertheless, and finally she said to God, "If You will heal me and extend my life I will follow your servant and hide away in hotel rooms and pray for him."

In Pasadena she prayed for two months for the success of the Southern Piedmont Crusade, before leaving for Greenville. She flew to the Greenville-Spartanburg Airport on March 1, and took a limousine to a hotel in Greenville. The next morning, as was her custom, she went out and asked a policeman to recommend a hotel for a "woman traveling alone." She moved into the Jack Tar Poinsett Hotel, where she had a room for the duration of the crusade.

Each day she went to Textile Hall between 4 and 5 P.M., well ahead of the crowds. First she prayed in the prayer room, and then she prayed in different parts of the sprawling steel and concrete building. Mrs. Goode said that when no one was looking she liked to pray at the evangelist's elevated stand.

Spurning publicity, she seeks to work quietly. Years ago members of the team would give her a special pass and occasionally invite her to sit on the platform, but she prefers to be just one of the crowd. During the sermon she prays for Billy, intensifying her prayers if she senses that he is tired or if he falters for a second.

"When the burden comes on me for the crusade, I can't go to sleep," she told Rowland, adding that she often prayed for hours through the night. "This battle is just as important as a battle in Viet Nam, and the boys in battle don't have time to go out and eat. I believe in hell — that you are going to one place or the other, so I work for lost souls, and that does away with these social functions."

Mrs. Goode said that she has ridden 47,000 miles on buses attending Crusades, and in recent years has traveled some by airplane. "I try not to bore fellow travelers, but if the opportunity presents itself I give my testimony." She starts with a simple testimony and then tells about Jesus and His love.

Relatives try to prevail upon her to stay at home and rest, she said, but she tells them, "I've got to go to these meetings until God takes this call off me." Her husband died more than 30 years ago and her two children live in California, are married and have families. She has eight grandchildren, most of whom are married, and ten great-grandchildren. "I don't go to a crusade until God provides the money for me," she said, adding that there are interesting stories about how the money comes to her. .

Although she has heard Billy Graham preach more times than anyone outside of the Graham organization, Mrs. Goode has never really talked to him. She worries about so many people taking up his time and wearing him out. Occasionally she will shake his hand and say nothing more than, "Billy, I love you."

"I believe in Mr. Graham with all my heart," she asserted. As she followed the evangelist from crusade to crusade, she has watched him change. He is growing constantly and his sermons get deeper and more meaningful. He is calmer now and paces the platform less than in earlier years.

Mrs. Goode is a "remarkable person, a devout Christian of deep faith," said Associate Crusade Director Haymaker, who has known her for many years. "Mr. Graham said that the one thing he needs most is prayer. Mrs. Goode is one of the champions of prayer."

On Saturday morning following the first night of the crusade the entire Executive Committee met at the Holiday Inn at a breakfast with the evangelist and other members of the Billy Graham team. It was a time of evaluation.

"I witnessed last night what I've never seen before," one committeeman exclaimed.

Following a period of informal testimony, Billy expressed appreciation for all that had been done by the Executive Committee in preparation for the crusade. He said he felt as if he were coming home in the crusade, and too, that it had a special meaning for him being in the home city of Cliff Barrows. He reported that buses were coming each night to the crusade from his home community of Black Mountain, N. C.[1]

Billy said he counted it a privilege to work with leaders in the area in the common task. "I believe we are going to see a flood-tide of the manifestation of God's spirit in our midst," he said. "The attitude among the workers is right, and I hope that ten days from now Billy Graham's name will not be on the lips of people, but rather Jesus Christ."

He does not understand any more than anyone else, he said, the amazing response shown in his crusades, and concluded that it was the work of the Holy Spirit.

The Rev. Walter H. Smith, director of the London Crusade, told briefly of preparations that had been made there.

A businessman at the breakfast said, "I have rededicated my life to Jesus Christ and feel that the Spirit of God is really in our midst."

---

[1]Don Bailey, general manager of radio station WFGW in Black Mountain, drove one of the buses daily to the crusade. The 50,000-watt station is a part of the Graham ministry. WMIT-FM, under the same management, transmits on 36,000 watts. Before becoming manager of the radio operations, Mr. Bailey was associated with the Graham film ministry.

# 8

"JESUS DEMANDS SELF-DENIAL, CROSS-BEARING, AND SACRIFICE OF His followers. It is not easy for a young person to be a Christian on the high school grounds or the university campus . . . Hundreds of you stand at the crossroads of your life. It is my prayer that you will decide for Christ no matter what the cost."

The words were those of Billy Graham, strong warrior of God, pointing the way, pleading earnestly in straightforward language with a vast audience made up largely of young people. It was the second night of the great crusade in Greenville, the first of four Youth Nights.

All of the 21,500 seats in the hall were taken and 3,500 people who could not be admitted stood outside, in near freezing weather, listening to the evangelist's message carried by loudspeakers.

"In spite of more conveniences, more entertainment, and more leisure, many psychologists and sociologists agree our teenagers are more miserable and unhappy than those of the last generation. Parents have communicated their purposelessness and meaningless of life and have failed their main function of making proper homes for their children. They also have failed to love them," he continued. "Drinking fathers and frug-dancing mothers are breeding a generation of unstable youngsters."

Reports of increased crime, demonstrations, revolts and relaxed morals are signs of "the teenage rampage," he said. "And the church has failed in its mission by giving the impression it is mainly for students of theology. Poor Sunday school teaching and the failure 'to talk straight from the shoulder' to the young people have compounded the problem. The schools have failed because they are so intent in imparting knowledge they do not direct students toward constructive goals."

"Christ is the answer," Billy Graham proclaimed, "but most young people prefer to be bystanders and are reluctant to be partisans for Christ."

At the outset Billy asked, "How many of you brought your Bibles? Hold them over your heads." Hands went up and Bibles were displayed all over the building. "Wonderful," he exclaimed. One man lifted a big family Bible aloft. The evangelist on the opening night had asked the people to bring their Bibles to the services.

In the first part of the service, the famous singer of spirituals and gospel songs, Ethel Waters, sang "His Eye Is On the Sparrow." A wave of emotion seemed to flow across the multitude in the hall as they sat almost motionless, some leaning forward on the edges of their seats, many standing on the back rows to get a better view of the singer. She had flown from her Pasadena, Calif., home to participate in the crusade.

During the preliminaries the evangelist left the platform and hall to speak briefly to the crowd outside for whom there were no seats. He apologized because they couldn't get in and told them that "we are working on some ways to enlarge the facilities next week."

"You don't have to be inside to make your decision for Christ," he told them. "You can make a decision right here. One of the greatest preachers I know was converted while standing in the rain outside Madison Square Garden in New York."

Before the evangelist returned to the main hall, several people made commitments and were assisted by counselors who were assigned to the outside. "God bless you," Billy said to each inquirer.

Jack Trim, *News* staff writer, recorded in a news story a few memorable scenes that followed:

The evangelist had walked through the hall on his way to the front entrance and shook hands with a number of teenagers and other youngsters who greeted him. One said, "Hi, Billy."

And that came close to setting the tone of the night's meeting. It was Youth Night and young people had come to listen to the address on "The Teen-Age Rampage."

He also autographed a small white Bible for a young girl who appeared extremely excited afterward.

The scene at the front door was one of eagerness and there were great sighs of relief as ushers finally let a few through at a time to take seats or stand in corners.

One woman came to ask the attendant with a loudspeaker to page her son from Clemson, for whom she was saving a seat, but the son did not answer and mom dashed back to her place.

One family was parted momentarily by the closing of the doors. The mother and a son made it inside, but father was left pressing against the glass. The boy, about nine years old, talked an usher into letting his father in.

Among those on the rostrum that night were U.S. Senator and Mrs. Donald Russell. The senator said he wanted "to welcome to the state Dr. Graham, a man who demonstrates so well the unique relevance of Christ to the world in which we live. We are so grateful for one who renews the faith and conviction of people in a day when they need spiritual strength as perhaps never before."

The giant choir, directed by Cliff Barrows, sang "This Is My Story," "There's a New Song in My Heart," "Since Jesus Came into My Heart." The audience joined in singing the last song.

Dr. Walter Smyth, a crusade director, read a portion of the 91st Psalm. Dr. Gordon Blackwell, Furman University president, extended a welcome to the throng. The opening prayer was given by the Rev. James Covington, pastor of Aldersgate Methodist Church. Further emphasis on youth was noted in the appearance on the program of Dr. Thomas L. Neely, president of North Greenville Junior College, chairman of the crusade Youth Committee, who read the Scripture.

Just before the message, Beverly Shea sang, "He's Got the Whole World in His Hands." Billy Graham's sermon was aimed principally at young people and when the invitation was given following the message, 850 went forward to profess their belief in Christ, walking to the pulpit area in front of the evangelist

The evangelist and young admirers (News-Piedmont photos)

Left to right: Graham, U.S. Senator Donald Russell
D-S.C.) and Crusade Chairman Dr. L. B. Johnson;
Below: enthusiastic choir members
(News-Piedmont photos)

from all parts of the auditorium. "Choose tonight," Billy pleaded, "the broad road or the narrow road . . . Heaven is waiting and the angels are watching . . . and the time for you is now. You have to choose . . . Turn to God while you can — before it is too late. Tonight may be the most important crossroads of your life."

The inquirers, a big majority of them high school and college students, filled the big open area in the front of the building and extended several yards along aisles as counselors worked swiftly, quietly trying to reach each individual. The steady, reassuring touch of the trained counselors was felt by the throng who had chosen God's way.

The evangelist was asked later about the turnout of so many young people at the crusade. "They are searching," he said. "They are asking deep questions: 'I'm involved in guilt. What can I do?' 'I'm not happy. I've got sex freedom, but I'm miserable. I feel guilty.' 'I've got to face death'."

"These are questions that they feel the church can answer," he added. "But often the church is answering questions nobody is asking. Students today are interested in any discussion of God and religion."

In the Youth Night audience were Mrs. Billy Graham, the Grahams' two sons, Franklin, 13, and Ned, 8, and attractive blonde daughter, Anne. They had driven down from Montreat that morning in time to join the Graham Team and others for lunch at the Barrows' home on Paris Mountain. They sat on a row near the front with Mrs. Cliff Barrows and three of her children, Betty Ruth, Buddy, and Bill.

It was Ned's first crusade and he gave rapt attention, once the service began. Before the service he left his seat and stepped outside the building for a moment. When he wanted to return he was stopped at the door, and it took a policeman to help get him past the ushers. As the choir rehearsed prior to the opening prayer, he made a few fine specimens of airplanes with the Crusade Newssheet distributed earlier, but restrained himself from flying them.

At the sermon's end, when his father gave the altar call, Ned and his brother went forward together to make public commitment to Christ.

Mrs. Graham and her children spent the night in the Barrows' guest cottage. A verbal exchange between the Graham boys the next morning was related by Mrs. Graham to illustrate that "when you accept Christ as your Saviour, you're not made godly overnight."

Ned thought that Franklin had infringed on his rights to a private bath. "That wasn't very godly," Ned commented. "You made a commitment to the Lord last night, but you don't act like it this morning."

"One of the great dangers for new Christians is discouragement," Mrs. Graham said at a Greenville Christian Woman's Club luncheon five weeks after the last Crusade service. "You are trying to put shoes on your faith. Possibly discouragement comes from expecting too much too soon."

Mrs. Graham, the former Ruth Bell, and her husband were graduated from Wheaton College in June 1943. They were married the following August. Today she looks more like a college girl than a mother of five children and a grandmother. Her eldest daughter, Mrs. Stephan Tchividjian, of Switzerland, has two children.

Mrs. Graham feels that "we mothers are homemakers by divine appointment and that we are put here to perform a divinely appointed task." She attends some of the services at most of the major crusades in America and spent the first two weeks of June at the 1966 London Crusade. But she feels that her place is in the home with the children and she spends most of the time at Montreat although her husband can be there very little.

"I'd rather see a little bit of Bill," she once said, "than a whole lot of any other man I know."

The Grahams live in a comfortable rustic home of hand-hewn logs, built in 1956 under Ruth's watchful eye. She searched old log cabins of the area for battered timbers to construct the house, which is designed for rest and relaxation. It nestles on a lofty perch overlooking valleys and mountain ridges.

Ruth Graham has long had ties with Greenville and since childhood has paid visits to her aunt, Mrs. D. L. Norris, on Paris Mountain just north of the city.

The planning and work of the Crusade Youth Committee, headed by Dr. Neely, the Junior College president, played a significant role leading to the tremendous youth response in the Southern Piedmont Crusade. Dr. Neely, a former Baptist missionary in Colombia and Venezuela (1942-53), tells here of some of the behind the scenes discussions, action and preparation for the history-making religious event:

"It was a blessing to work as chairman of the Youth Committee. Other than the Executive Committee, this committee had the first public meeting of any kind in connection with the crusade. On November 22, 1965, representatives from all of the colleges in upper South Carolina and a few in the Piedmont area of North Carolina were invited to Greenville for a banquet. The presidents of these colleges had been written, asking that they name some faculty member as co-ordinator on their campus. These faculty members, with two student leaders from each campus, were invited.

"We were overwhelmed by their response, since there had been no publicity about the crusade. Johnny Lenning and Forrest Layman presented ideas for use on the campus in preparation for the crusade. Each representative was urged to carry these ideas back and to put them into practice immediately at the colleges. Many colleges participated, providing young people for the crusade choir and for counseling service. Many colleges had prayer groups that met for months before the crusade began.

"The Youth Committee, with Johnny Lenning, Forrest Layman, and Willis Haymaker, also worked among high schools. Due to much emphasis on separation of church and state in this area at the time, because the S. C. Baptist Convention had rejected Furman University's desire to receive a Federal grant, we found it necessary to be very cautious in working with high schools. One idea that we worked on intensely but which never materialized, was the plan to have an afternoon service with Dr. Graham speaking in Textile Hall to high school students. It was thought that there might be a possibility of this being the first public meeting in the crusade. We found encouragement and promise of cooperation from many school leaders, but decided against holding this service. The contacts and work done in connection with this stimulated much interest among high school officials and students. As a result, instead of having one afternoon service for high school students, we had four

Mr. and Mrs. Graham,
deplaning for a crusade.

Virginia Leftwich Graham
(oldest daughter of Billy
Graham) and Stephen
Tchividjian of Switzerland
before their marriage in
1963. They now have
two children.

The Graham family at their mountain home in Montreat.

wonderful youth nights during the crusade. Two came after the crusade went into dual services, thus giving six youth services.

"I can testify to the impact the crusade made on the college [North Greenville Junior] where I serve. Some nights during the crusade over half of our student body were present. More than sixty students drove fourteen miles to Greer to take counseling classes and served as crusade counselors. Over seventy students and faculty members sang in the choir. Faculty members and students served as ushers, and on key committees. Two faculty members were on the Advisory Committee.

"Groups of four girls to a suite in our dormitories started praying for the crusade months before it began. Never was there a vesper service or morning watch in which the crusade was not remembered in prayer. In the Men's dormitory, small groups gathered to pray. The prayer services have continued and have been amplified since the meeting closed. When the crusade telecasts began, intense prayer was made by our students that God might bless the programs.

"One thrilling personal satisfaction that I received from the crusade was in connection with the selection of the people to give testimonies and sing. I remember one day in the crusade headquarters when a small group of us were talking about the Youth Nights, trying to select a special soloist or people to bring testimonies. Various names were mentioned, among them Steve Sloan and Bill Glass, who did come.

"I was impressed to mention the name of Myrtle Hall whom I had heard sing on radio but had not met. I had talked to a number of people, however, who knew her and who said that she was a consecrated Christian. At this particular time we needed some young Negro to have an important part in this crusade, and I felt it ought to be a local one if possible. I stated frankly that I thought we ought to invite her, and that I would especially like to see her appear since she was from Greenville.

"The suggestion was received well by the group there, and passed on to the team. When I heard that she was to sing, I experienced a real thrill — and an even greater one when the actual time came. Later, when I heard the telecasts, it seemed that her effectiveness was even greater on TV than it was in Textile Hall. I believe that God will use her life to influence thousands to accept Christ as Saviour.

"For some time prior to the actual beginning of the services, I had a strong feeling that Textile Hall would not be large enough. I had thought about many ideas without mentioning them to anyone. Also, I prayed intensely that God would direct the leadership to know what to do if crowds overflowed the hall. When the first service began on Friday night, the building was almost packed to capacity. I knew that by the weekend there would not be space for the people, and that thousands would have to be turned away.

"That night announcement was made to the Executive Committee of a breakfast the next morning at the Holiday Inn with Dr. Graham and the Team. I felt that the breakfast was called for us to face the problem of seating and to decide what could be done. Although it was a meeting that I will never forget because the Spirit of God was upon it, it was given over entirely to prayer and testimonies. Nothing was said about provisions for an overflow crowd.

"When I was in my automobile and on my way back to the campus, I felt an unusual burden that this problem had to be dealt with, and dealt with quickly. I thought about the possibility of closed circuit TV in the Furman auditorium or in Wade Hampton High School. Then the idea came that perhaps a tent could be set on the airport near Textile Hall. I knew that a real solution would be an extra service each night, but I took it for granted that the health of Dr. Graham would not permit this.

"When I arrived on campus, no one was in the office, since we were in spring holidays. Immediately I plugged in a direct line to my office and called Dr. L. D. Johnson. He was out, but I left word to have him call me immediately. I sat in the office unable to work, and only able to pray that God would direct us in this challenge. Finally Dr. Johnson called, and I laid the burden of my problem upon him as Chairman of the Executive Committee. I even mentioned an evangelist who was not cooperating with the crusade but who owned a large tent, and offered to go see him. Dr. Johnson promised to work on the problem immediately, and to report the outcome. I felt greatly relieved that someone was working on the problem. At three that afternoon, Dr. Johnson called to tell me that he had talked with Dr. Graham and Cliff Barrows. He said that both

agreed that we perhaps would have overflow crowds and would
have to do something.

"After the service that night, and the auditorium was filled
and several thousand had to be turned away, everybody knew
that something must be done. The Arrangements Committee,
together with Dr. Johnson, explored many ideas. A building
near Textile Hall was looked at and found unsuitable.

"Sometime during the weekend Dr. Graham decided that
the solution was two services a night, and agreed to it. What
a great thrill it was when we could announce that beginning
Wednesday there would be double services. All of us learned
what a great God we have. When the Executive Committee
had voted to buy 20,000 chairs, some people thought we were
out of our minds. Little did we dream that most of those chairs
would be filled twice daily for the last five days of the crusade."

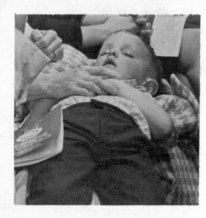

Young members of the crusade audience
Dr. Graham addressing overflow crowd
outside Hall (News-Piedmont photos)

# 9

BEFORE NOON ON SUNDAY, MARCH 6, CARS TURNING FROM SIX-LANE Pleasantburg Drive into streets leading to Textile Hall made steady streams of traffic, and no one doubted that all of the 21,500 seats in the auditorium would be taken long before the 3:30 crusade service. Some early arrivals brought lunch.

A woman entered a phone booth at 1:30 and made a call. "You might as well stay at home," she told the person on the other end. "There are enough people standing outside to fill the place twice."

Groups had arrived by buses from as far away as Bristol, Va., Macon, Ga., Charleston, S. C. Mrs. Maxwell Kinsey and others came nearly 200 miles from Ehrhardt, S. C., to join relatives and friends at the service. Mr. and Mrs. Willard S. Sharitz arrived from Wytheville, Va., to spend a week's vacation in Greenville to attend the crusade.

Entrances to the hall were opened to the public at 2 P.M. and the people surged in until the hall was filled. Then the doors had to be closed. A crowd estimated by police at 6,000 was left outside to hear the service carried on loud-speakers.

Crusade planners were overjoyed at the turnout, growing larger daily, but realized that something would have to be done to accommodate the people.

As he had done on Saturday night, Billy appeared before the overflow crowd and said he was sorry that everyone could not get inside, adding that "about twice as many people came as we had figured. I am proud that so many people want to come."

"It makes no difference where you stand," he continued. "You can receive Christ right here in this street. Maybe God has sent you to this place for a reason. Repent where you are and let Christ come into your heart."

Scores of hands went up when he asked if any wanted to commit themselves to the Lord and His way.

In the pulpit later the evangelist's first words were of regret "for the thousands standing outside who could not be admitted. We never dreamed so many would come. We had hoped the building would be filled by the end of the crusade." He explained that Textile Hall is the third or fourth largest auditorium in the United States.

Billy preached that night on "The End of the World," taking his text from II Peter 3:2-13, that tells of a world which overflowed with water and "perished," and warns that the world will be consumed by fire "against the day of judgment and perdition of ungodly men."

Clearly, forcefully he spoke, pacing slowly across the rostrum, his arms waving in dramatic gestures. "We should realize that in delaying the day of judgment God is extending His grace to us because he loves us," he continued. "But the day of the Lord will come as a thief in the night — no one will have advance notice. The heavens shall pass away with a great noise and elements shall melt with fervent heat, the earth also and the works therein shall be burned up."

"Science has made possible the end of the world," he said, "and the greatest threats are not the hydrogen and atomic bombs, but the germs and gases that can be loosed to sweep the world. These are in the arsenals of several nations."

The evangelist said he had more to go on than Noah did. "Noah had no scientific evidence that the flood was coming, but God had said it and so Noah believed it. I accept the word of God, too. I believe in my Bible, but I have no scientific evidence that the end of the world is coming."

Four hundred fifty-seven persons responded to the invitation after the sermon, walking down the aisles to the front of the packed hall. Singly and in couples they came, a husband often following in his wife's steps. There were snow-thatched heads and little boys with brush cuts, a father and a little girl, a teen-age boy and girl making the walk together.

Bowed heads were lifted to hear the evangelist, who was beginning to speak to the inquirers.

"When you came forward tonight, you came to receive Christ. You did it by faith. Perhaps you feel that your faith is not very strong, but Christ said you only need faith the size of a grain of mustard seed to begin. Now you will need to get into your Bibles and start to grow. Standing beside you is a counselor to show you how . . . ."

A special guest at the service was U. S. Senator J. Strom Thurmond, who was introduced by James B. Orders, Jr., co-chairman of the Crusade Committee. "In this day, when crime and political pressures make the future precarious," the Senator said, "the country needs Billy Graham more than ever."

Dr. Akbar Abdul Haqq, associate evangelist on the Graham team, who had preached that morning in the First Baptist Church, gave the opening prayer. He and some of the other team members were presented by Billy. They included: Dr. Grady Wilson and Dr. T. W. Wilson, boyhood friends of the evangelist and long-time associates; the Rev. Howard Jones and the Rev. Leighton Ford, Billy's brother-in-law.

Ethel Waters, in buoyant spirit and gracious smiles, sang, "Oh, How I Love Jesus," and immediately before the evan-gelist preached, Bev Shea added musical strength and appeal with his solo, "Green Pastures."

The music of the blended voices of the choir, men in white shirts and dark trousers, women in white blouses and dark skirts, rolled through the concrete building. Cliff Barrows seemed to have put his whole heart and soul into directing the choir, which included hundreds of his townspeople. "The con-crete ceiling, lower than in many large auditoriums, seemed just right for the choir," Cliff said later. "The music just rolls out." The choir had been put together before the start of the crusade by another well-known musician and singer, DuPre Rhame, pro-fessor of music and director of fine arts at Furman University since 1933, who served as chairman of the Crusade Music Committee.

Max McGee Rice, chairman of the Crusade Visitation Committee, read the Scripture. The Rev. James T. Sheely, pastor of the Greenville Church of God and chairman of the Groups Reservations Committee, gave the offertory prayer and the Rev. William W. McNeill, pastor of St. Matthew's Methodist Church, gave the benediction.

In a far corner in the balcony sat the deaf. The words of Billy Graham were carried to them through interpreters, their hands and arms gracefully gesticulating in the mute sign language. A count showed 112 people in that section Sunday afternoon. The words of the sermon, songs and other messages were relayed to the deaf throughout the service, and tingles of excitement were observed in the section.

"Dr. Graham has a marvelous way of getting people in a spiritual mood," said Jack Green, a high school senior who served as one of the translators, "and I felt it was my responsibility to get the deaf in the same mood. I regarded it as my responsibility to put Dr. Graham's feeling into sign language," he added. "It's hard to explain how you can put feeling into signs, but if you don't have a feeling for it you can't do it. You'd just be putting out words."

When Billy gave the Sunday invitation, a 25-year-old deaf mother of two small children walked from the balcony, down the wide stairway and along the main floor aisles, joining the throng of others streaming forward from all over Textile Hall. She made her way to a point where a counselor familiar with the sign language was stationed. Standing nearby was the Rev. R. C. Eustace, pastor of Reedy Creek Baptist Church in Greenville County, who was asked by the interpreter to assist in counseling the deaf inquirer.

"Through the interpreter, the woman and I talked for several minutes," Mr. Eustace related to his congregation the following Sunday. "She accepted Christ as her personal Saviour right there in Textile Hall. She wept for joy that she had been converted. There was no doubt in my mind about it being a real experience."

Because she could not hear and had no way of knowing what went on and was said in churches of her community, Mr. Eustace said, she did not attend church services. "But I am happy to report now," Mr. Eustace related, "that arrangements have been worked out with the pastor of a church near her home in Laurens County for sign language interpretation for her." The woman said she wanted to be baptized and become a church member.

Before the crusade ended, others went forward from Section 169 (reserved for the deaf) to make a profession of faith in Christ.

The advisor to the deaf for the Crusade was the Rev. M. M. Rabon of Easley, and Mrs. Joyce Smith was chief interpreter. They were assisted by young Jack Green, both of whose parents are deaf; Miss Julie Evatt of Anderson, a student at Furman University, and Miss Bonnie Coleman, a student at T. L. Hanna High School in Anderson. Miss Nell Peyton of Asheville, N. C., who conducts a television program for the deaf, spoke with signs for evangelist Graham on the opening night of the crusade.

A blind man and his seeing eye dog were at more than one Crusade service.

Not all who braved the crowds to hear the minister of Christ's great evangelical pleas came on their own feet, or with bodies whole and strong. In wheel chairs and on crutches came many with joyous hearts despite their infirmities.

Faltering physically, they possibly had greater need to seek out and find strength greater than their own, strength and power that encompasses hope, devotion, faith. A special vantage point was set aside for wheelchairs. In the final moments of exhortation, some moved forward, with gentle assistance, into the circle of the committed.

The Greenville Chapter of the American National Red Cross set up a first aid station in Textile Hall and treated 324 persons for various illnesses and minor injuries during the ten days of the crusade.

On Sunday's "Hour of Decision" radio broadcast, heard by 25,000,000 listeners tuned to 990 stations, Billy devoted his message to the theme that "senseless slaughter on the highways is a spiritual problem. Christians," he said, "have a definite obligation to drive carefully and safely on the highways."

"If the present rate of killing on the highways continues," he warned, "half of all Americans will someday be killed or injured in an automobile accident."

Even the blind (left) and deaf (below)
and the "halt" heard the Word
(News-Piedmont photo)

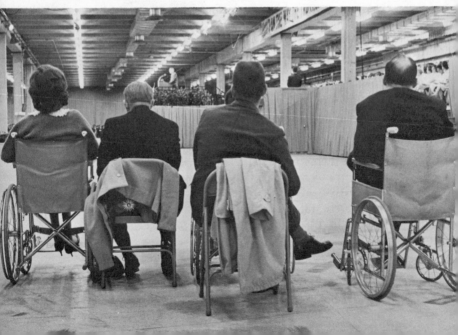

"Where are the protesters? Where are the demonstrators? Where are the marchers? If ever there was a problem in this country that needed discussion, debate and protest, it is the slaughter on the highways."

Breaking the golden rule — "Do unto others what you would have them do unto you" — and the commandment "Thou shalt not kill" account for many accidents, he said. Other causes are selfishness, showing off, becoming angry, carelessness and drunkenness.

"Thus the major problem of highway safety is not speed, a faulty car, a bad tire, or a bad highway — the problem is man himself. The cure for the slaughter on the highways is a spiritual rebirth gained by repenting of your sins and receiving Christ as your Saviour."

# 10

To a well-known Anderson clergyman, the Rev. Edwin B. Clippard, rector of Grace Episcopal Church, the crusade brought an unusual experience.

"I was strangely moved to go forward" when Billy Graham gave the invitation, he related. "Something just propelled me . . . and I was out of my seat and down the aisle . . . The significant thing about this is that a relevant healing took place in me."

The experience had its beginning a few hours before the service when he attended a special Greenville showing of "The Restless Ones," the Billy Graham movie, which impressed him as "one of the most profound statements of the problem of parents and teenagers, each for the other, and the relevance of faith in that situation."

As the film was shown, "something gripped me and moved me," he said. "I was tremendously touched."

Counselors were not on hand and an invitation was not given as during the regular runs that followed in Greenville, Spartanburg, Anderson and other places. When the lights went on at the end of the show, however, those who wanted to give themselves to Christ or rededicate their lives were asked to raise their hands.

The feeling came over him that he should raise his hand. At the same time he thought, *This is a silly thing for me to do. Here I have been a confessing Christian for years. Here I am,*

*a priest of the church, one to whom ordination has been given,
the terrifically serious problem of handing communion to people
and pronouncing absolution and blessing. I know that my acts
have been used by the Holy Spirit. Why should this happen
to me?*

A friend connected with the showing of "The Restless Ones"
advised him to attend the Crusade service that afternoon and
go forward in response to the invitation. So Mr. Clippard
stayed over in Greenville and attended the first of the day's
dual services. His faith was almost shaken before the service,
he recalled later, by the "yakety-yak-yak" of a former acquaintance who had defected to a "peculiar, offbeat sect" and who
had driven more than 200 miles to hear Billy Graham's message.

Mr. Clippard sat next to an elderly woman he had known
years before in Columbia, a devout Christian, and he told her
of his warm experience at the showing of the movie, and his
reaction to the words of the woman who had joined the
"peculiar sect."

"Well, don't let what she says upset a beautiful experience
for you," the woman next to him said.

Throughout the Graham sermon, Mr. Clippard listened in-
tently. He was stirred deeply and felt compelled to respond
to the evangelist's invitation. Here are the words of Mr.
Clippard:

"I was strangely moved to go forward. The same thoughts
I had that morning went through my mind again — why in the
world should this be; what can this accomplish? I know that
my Redeemer liveth; I know that I have lived in Him for a long
time. Wherein, what was the purpose? Why was the Spirit
moving me to just come forward?

"Then all at once, something just propelled me out of my
seat and I was out of my seat and down the aisle. I had a very
happy conversation with a layman, a businessman serving as a
counselor. He was concerned that I had not believed before,
and it seemed he had difficulty understanding that it was not
a matter of not believing, but was in fact something else and
I was very happy about it.

"Now the significant thing about this is that a very relevant
healing took place in me. I have always been a coward, just
the worst kind. I have heard of people who have never been

afraid. I am sure that one of the great problems in my personality has been this certain timidity. The amazing thing is that by consenting to go through with this physical witnessing of the faith, there was a healing within me that was tremendous. I believe that we always have room to grow. If we are not having new spiritual experiences, something is wrong with us."

Mr. Clippard, tall and distinguished in appearance, has been in the clergy for two decades. He studied law and would have practiced that profession had he not entered the seminary to become a priest. His wife is a daughter of the late Dr. D. D. Wallace, long-time Wofford College professor and noted South Carolina historian.

A Greenville manufacturing company executive, Robert R. Gibson, tells a lucid story of his crusade experience.

"I have enjoyed a happier, better life since I allowed Jesus to come into my life," he said. "The Graham message was right for Bob Gibson and it's been right for a lot of other Bob Gibsons that I know."

"Billy Graham asked, 'Is Christ in your heart?' He wasn't in mine, but he is today," Mr. Gibson said. "That was the message of the crusade. It is very simple."

Mr. Gibson was brought up in a Christian home, has a Christian wife and is the father of three school-age children. They all have long attended church services and participated in church programs.

"But worldly things influenced me greatly," he said. "I traveled the cocktail circuit and thought it was all right. I didn't have to find much of an excuse to take a drink."

He began taking another look at his life when his oldest son, Larry, now 14, became interested in church work and dedicated himself to Christ.

"I couldn't come around to giving up my 'good times,' however," Mr. Gibson continued.

As the Billy Graham Crusade neared and a call was made in his church for ushers, he volunteered to serve. He and his family attended several crusade services, and Mr. Gibson was assigned to usher at both services on Friday night.

"I didn't feel enthusiastic about it and Friday afternoon I decided to go on home from work and forget about the crusade," he related. "But an unusual thing happened. As I drove on my way home, when I reached 291 By-Pass, which leads to Textile Hall, a sudden compelling urge came on me to continue on to the crusade, rather than turn into the street that leads to my home. I simply couldn't go home. I felt that I must proceed to Textile Hall."

Was God's hand leading him to the crusade? Billy Graham had said at an earlier service that no one in the audience was there by accident; all came by God's purpose.

Mr. Gibson went to Textile Hall and assisted in ushering. Throughout the service he felt that the altar was beckoning him. When the invitation was given at the second service he got out of his seat and started to the front. For a few seconds he thought of walking to the door and leaving the building, but God was walking with him, he said, and the altar was the place to go. There he committed himself to Christ.

No longer bewildered or unsure, he experienced a comfort he had never known before, and he drove home as rapidly as traffic would allow, to reveal to his family the happy news of his decision for the Lord. Their hearts lifted by the developments, they had family devotions in their home that night for the first time, reading Scripture and praying together.

Months later, Mr. Gibson said: "I may become a backslider, I hope not, I pray not, but since the crusade I have known what the better life is.

"I enjoy church work more; I love reading the Bible, I want to know more, to study more. Even singing means more to me. I can sing better. This may sound strange: I can stay on key better. I believe the words, I believe the story.

"I will shout from the housetops that believing in Jesus Christ as the son of God is the answer for the United States, for England, for the world, for everybody. This is the message of the crusade, the message of the cross."

Here are some other testimonies of what the crusade meant.

G. H., of West Columbia, S. C., wrote: "Tonight I watched for the second time the televised services from the crusade in Greenville. I was converted March 9 at the first early evening service at Textile Hall, so this crusade has a very special meaning for me. My wife was converted as a result of one of your television broadcasts about two years ago. Our life together has never been happier."

James Thomas, a truck driver of Piedmont, S. C., told of feeling the outpouring of God's power in Textile Hall. "I surrendered my life to Him on the first night of the crusade," he said.

From then on attending crusade services became a habit with him. He didn't miss a day; in fact, he went an extra day! Here's the way Mr Thomas related it:

"After work I went straight home, bathed and dressed for the service, and drove to Textile Hall early to be among the first arrivals, just as I had done every day from the start.

"It was the afternoon of Monday, March 15, and I knew I would be there early, but I began to wonder when no other cars were turning into the roads leading to Textile Hall. I parked and had the entire parking area just about to myself. Then it dawned on me that I had been to the crusade for ten days and that the last service had been held the day before — on Sunday.

"I had enjoyed the crusade so much, I was sorry that it had ended. I took my time in leaving the parking area, just tarried and praised God for his wonderful blessings."

Mr. Thomas said at mid-summer that his life had been changed and that he treasured the experience of the crusade. "It has lasted," he said.

A hospital employee residing more than 50 miles from Greenville, a pretty young woman whose long-time lukewarm attitude toward religion evolved into a yearning for spiritual growth, felt a strong desire to attend the Crusade. Unable to induce any of her family or friends to take her or accompany her to hear Billy Graham, she made the trip alone although it involved a late hour return on a lonely highway.

It was Youth Night and the evangelist preached to a capacity audience made up largely of young people. Young people are confronted by problems with which they are unable to cope, he said, and because of this they often make havoc of their lives. He spoke of the forgiveness of the Heavenly Father, pointing out that many people need Jesus because of their immorality, pride, jealousy, envy.

When he called on his listeners to come forward to ask God's forgiveness for their sins and to begin a new life, the young

woman moved quickly to the aisle and then to the front of the
hall, one of the first to respond to the evangelist's invitation.

She had driven alone to Greenville, and at the service she
knew no one she saw. When she went forward, she told an
understanding counselor, the loneliness did not disappear, but
lost its sting. She had made a decision for God, she said, and
wanted to dedicate her life to Christian service.

After her convincing and satisfying experience with God,
she related later to her counselor, she drove home unafraid,
happy in the belief that she had found forgiveness and peace.
In the weeks that followed she and the counselor kept in touch
by mail and telephone, and in mid-summer the young hospital
employee revealed an intense hunger to become a servant of
God as a foreign missionary. Soon afterward a medical missionary on furlough called on her, first at the hospital and then at
her home, and talked of the challenge of this field of ministry
and service for God.

The grace of God at work in the Southern Piedmont Crusade
touched the lives of convicts in the South Carolina State Penitentiary and inmates of Harbison Correctional Institution for
Women at Columbia.

From the two prisons buses came to the crusade on sepa-
rate nights, bringing prisoners who asked to hear Billy Graham
preach. As they arrived at Textile Hall they were greeted and
welcomed by members of the Good Neighbor Sunday school
class of the Greenville First Presbyterian Church, who also
served them box lunches.

The convicts wore their prison uniforms, topped by long
coats, sweaters, or car coats. The women inmates, attending
services the night following the men, were dressed in civilian
clothes.

"This is my first trip out into society in fifteen years," said
a Negro convict sitting in the auditorium before the service
began. "I've been behind that wall for an armed robbery fifteen
years ago, and I've almost completed my sentence. I'm starting
a new life and I don't want to hide anything."

He was one of forty-seven men from the Penitentiary attending the Crusade at their own request. All were nearing the end

of their terms and were in a special program of the institution designed to prepare prisoners for a return to society.

"I went to prison when I was seventeen and I'm thirty-two now," the convict explained as he sat awaiting Billy Graham to step to the platform and begin the service. "A lot of things I saw from the bus coming to Greenville today have changed. I want to start again and I think this [the crusade] will help me. I've heard him [Billy Graham] speak on television, and I know he's helped people in other cities."

A white prisoner said he was looking forward to leading a new life once his penitentiary term is completed. "This crusade is a spark to some of us," he said. "Let's hope some of us will grow from it."

Col. William M. Campbell, superintendent of the Penitentiary's pre-release center, accompanied the men on the bus trip from Columbia and sat with them. Sitting near Col. Campbell, a trusty serving two years for robbery said that a weakness for drinking had kept him from being a Christian and had led to crime. "I think I've learned my lesson and it won't be hard for me now to look at a bottle and pass it up," he volunteered. "I don't want to be on alcohol ever again. Maybe tonight I'll find what I'm looking for."

That night in Textile Hall six of the prisoners went forward and stood with other penitents to receive Christ. The trusty who felt that he had overcome his drinking problem was one. The Negro who had been imprisoned nearly fifteen years was another.

Returning to Columbia some of the men talked about the sermon, talked of eternal life and of their intention to follow the "straight and narrow path." "There was quite a bit of discussion" as the prisoners traveled back on the bus, Col. Campbell related later. "The reaction was just fabulous. They talked more about Dr. Graham's message than anything else."

Back at the Penitentiary the new "attitude or outlook on life" of the group attending the crusade service was noticeable, Col. Campbell said. "Their morale is better, and it's having a good effect around the institution," he added.

It was the first time inmates had left the Penitentiary to participate in such a meeting. Inside the prison, religious services are held regularly, on Sundays and Tuesdays.

Miss Ethel Waters thrilled crusade audiences with her
songs and testimony  (News-Piedmont  photo)

A few weeks after the prisoners made the 200-mile trip, each received a copy of the Billy Graham Bible as a gift from the Good Neighbor Class. The idea of the class sponsoring the prisoners was originated by Mrs. W. Harrell Wilson, a well-known Greenville resident who was "thinking about people who should attend the crusade and probably wanted to be there." A number of the inmates wrote to the class to express their appreciation and some said they received spiritual nourishment to help them travel the road ahead straight.

Reporter Frances Evans of the *Greenville Piedmont,* who talked to Col. Campbell in Columbia following the crusade service, wrote: "One thing that impressed the inmates," Col. Campbell said, "was the fact that they were treated as 'people, not as a bunch of convicts'."

Thirty-five women from the correctional institution, their ages ranging from 21 to 65, sat in a body in the crusade hall after eating the lunches given them by the Good Neighbor Class. An unexpected treat for the group came when Ethel Waters stepped down from the platform to the main floor before the service started and waved and smiled at them. They acknowledged and returned the greetings by nodding their heads and smiling. Mrs. Langdon Ligon, Jr., of Greenville had gone to the platform and asked Miss Waters if she would wave to the women from the platform. "I'll do more than that," the 70-year-old singer said, "I'll go down there and welcome them."

The women prisoners were part of a capacity audience listening to a heart-searching Youth Night message and the evangelist's plea to put God first. They heard songs of praise and faith by the massive crusade choir and solos by Bev Shea and Miss Waters.

"You are not redeemed at a bargain," Billy said. "You are not redeemed with silver and gold, the Bible says, but with the precious blood of Jesus Christ . . . Let your mind stay on Christ and then you will have peace."

While organist Don Hustad played a muted hymn, the evangelist gave the invitation in quiet, moving words: "Let Jesus come into your heart and change your life. Let Him forgive your sins. You can make a decision tonight that will change your life . . . Get up and come and receive Jesus Christ."

Now the choir hummed with the organ music. It was a time of decision and the aisles between the rows of folding chairs were thick with people pacing to the front from all over the auditorium. One of the prisoners stood up, slipped to the end of the row and joined the throng moving forward. She was followed by another, then another.

Mrs. Dorothy J. DuBose, who accompanied the inmates on the trip, reported that thirteen of the thirty-five in the group went forward and were counseled. The counselors expressed their belief that there would be new witnesses for God within the walls of the women's prison.

Returning to Columbia that night, the women spoke of the crusade, of their experiences, the people they saw, and they sang from the crusade songbooks given to them by the Good Neighbor Class. At the end of the trip they joined in rendering a number composed during the bus trip. It included these words: "Thank you, Mrs. DuBose, for helping make our dreams come true."

Within a short time all of the prisoners who attended the Graham services wrote thank-you notes or letters to their benefactors, the members of the Sunday school class. Like the Penitentiary prisoners, the women inmates received Billy Graham Bibles and began reading them.

From a seat on the platform behind the evangelist's rostrum, Dr. Wallace Fridy, the Anderson co-chairman of the Crusade, watched the lines of solemn-faced people coming forward in response to Billy Graham's invitation at the close of his sermon.

"It was an inspiring scene," Dr. Fridy said. "Young and old came. Husbands and wives made the walk together. Many came with great weight of guilt, and many just wanting to rededicate themselves to Jesus Christ. After the group assembled I copied down what Dr. Graham said. He told them to do four things:

1. Read the Gospel of John five times, and read the Bible every day;
2. Spend at least 15 minutes every day in prayer. Just talk to the Lord. Confess your sins: Thank Him for life and all that He does for you;
3. Witness for Him: How do you do this? Simply by a smile on your face, by being kind to everyone you meet, by being gracious and honest in all your dealings with men. Be honest in school — don't cheat; fill your life with integrity;

4. Get into the Church; there is no such thing as a perfect Church for it is made up of redeemed sinners; get active and be faithful to the Church.

"After his brief counsel, he asked the group to repeat after him this prayer:

"O God, I am a sinner. I am sorry for my sins. I am willing to turn from them, to change my course. I receive Jesus Christ as my Saviour. I confess Him as Lord of my life. From this moment on I want to follow Him in the fellowship of the Church."

"There will perhaps never be such a crusade again in our lifetime in this area. This man, Billy Graham, is certainly being used by God in a unique way in our generation. He is a living example of what can happen in the life of a man, when he gives himself completely to God."

Two missionaries who have spent much of their lives in Africa in the service of the Master attended the crusade services daily. Miss Mary S. Beam and Miss A. Elizabeth Cridland have prayed for Billy Graham and his ministry since they heard him in Madison Square Garden in 1957.

In 1965, after serving in the Sudan for a quarter of a century, they were ousted on political counts. Coming back to the States, they made their home in Greenville until leaving in June 1966 for a new assignment in Somalia. Volunteering their services to the crusade team, Miss Beam and Miss Cridland became crusade workers in the counselor follow-up program.

Before leaving Sudan they completed a translation of the New Testament into the language of the Uduk tribe and this has been published by the American Bible Society. They were permitted to turn their properties over to the Sudanese pastor they had educated and trained and left to carry on the Christian work, and to him they sent clippings of the newspaper coverage of the Southern Piedmont Crusade.

Three dozen residents of Memphis, Tenn., traveled 525 miles to Greenville and attended four crusade services. The trip was arranged by Mr. and Mrs. J. W. Ware, who accompanied groups to earlier crusades in New York, Chicago, Los Angeles and other places.

Through the crusade trip, long separated relatives were brought together when one of the Memphis party, Mrs. Dell McClure, visited her Greenville aunt, Mrs. W. H. Ballenger, Jr. They had not seen each other for 34 years.

Traveling the greatest distance to the crusade was an associate evangelist of the Billy Graham team, the Rev. Howard Jones, who flew from Liberia.

One week before the Southern Piedmont Crusade opened Mr. Jones, a Negro minister, was in Ghana. He had been conducting two months of evangelistic meetings and was in the capital, Accra, when the military overthrew the pro-communist Premier Nkrumah. Mr. Jones had to pass a picket line to get out of the country.

"I had to face up to my own preaching when the soldiers rounded us up for search," he said. "I had been delivering messages of faith during times of suffering, trials and persecution, and it came my turn to practice what I had been preaching."

There was little armed conflict connected with the overthrow, but the gunfire put foreigners in Accra on notice they could be in for a hard time.

"Africa is in crisis and this is a time for evangelism there," Mr. Jones asserted, adding that he was heartened by the great response in Ghana and other countries to Christian ministry and by the evident hunger for God.

Mr. Jones lives half of the year in Long Island, N. Y., and the other half in Monrovia, Liberia. He and two other ministers and a singer work in Africa with Operation African Ministry, sponsored by the Billy Graham Evangelistic Association.

# 11

THE PRESENT GENERATION OF YOUNG PEOPLE MAY BE THE MOST religious-minded in American history, Billy Graham has said. Services on four of the ten crusade days were aimed at challenging them with the Gospel of Christ. On several nights he asked: "How many of you are under 25 years of age?" The young people were in the majority each time, and on Youth Nights their total ran as high as 70 per cent.

During the crusade Billy Graham's messages to young people were underscored by testimonies from nationally known football stars. Steve Sloan, quarterback for the Atlanta Falcons, introduced by the evangelist as a "young man who has been touched by God," said he asks God to help him do his best before every game he plays. He spoke at the Monday night service.

Three nights later Bill Glass, defensive end for the Cleveland Browns, stood before a multitude and told what God means to him and of his decision at 17 to follow Jesus Christ.

Standing tall and walking in the way they feel that Jesus would have them walk as an example to thousands of American youth today, Sloan, Glass and others like them have brought incalculable inspiration to young people. These young athletes, with other special guests, sat on the platform overlooking the rectangular Crusade hall and saw rivers of people, some adults with the throngs of youths, make their way forward at the time of decision.

Steve Sloan, who was All-American quarterback at the University of Alabama before he was drafted by Atlanta, said he committed his life to Christ when he was a sophomore in high school. He heard a speaker at a retreat ask, "What if your game of life were played back to God tonight? Would you lose?" The question struck home, he said, and he knew he needed to change his life if he was to win in the game of life.

"There's one thing I regret since I became a Christian," he admitted. "I've let God down so many times, but He's never let me down one time. You just have to look up, to reach up, and He's there ready to help you."

Introduced that night also was Mike Fair of Greenville, the University of South Carolina's outstanding quarterback, who is recognized for his Christian work. His coach is Paul Dietzel, who became known as "God's man at West Point" when he coached at the U. S. Military Academy.

*News* Sports Editor Jim Anderson, wrote this in his "Top of the Morning" column about an interview with Sloan:

> Steve Sloan has twice known elation beyond what one usually experiences.
> One was a football victory for Alabama's All American quarterback.
> The other time was attending a Billy Graham Crusade at Montgomery.
> Steve, here last night to appear for the local Graham Crusade, described those feelings.
> He was an obscure third team quarterback his sophomore year when Alabama met Ole Miss in the Sugar Bowl. Coach Bear Bryant started Sloan against the favored Rebels and Steve directed the Tide to a stunning 12-7 victory.
> "I've had a lot of 'em," Steve said of football thrills, "but I was more excited after that game than any other. Because I was a sophomore, I suppose. But I remembered how I felt right after that game."
> Steve was driving by himself from Montgomery to Tuscaloosa after attending his first Graham Crusade.
> "I don't ever remember feeling that good," he recalls of his experience in hearing Billy Graham. "Just to hear Dr. Graham!

"I drove along singing . . . kinda half-way embarrassed, but no one else could hear me sing."

On the night Steve Sloan spoke at Textile Hall 860 inquirers registered decisions. Bill Glass, appearing at dual services, saw 554 go forward at the first service and 759 at the second when Billy Graham called for commitments to Christ.

Glass was introduced as a "six-foot, four-inch, 240-pound man who loves God with all of his heart." The athlete related that once his young son, Bobby, in reply to a reprimand from a neighbor, said, "Do you know who my dad is?" Bobby, in the next breath, answered with these surprising words: "My father is a Christian." The neighbor thought the boy would have reminded him that his father was a big strong athlete.

Glass told the crusade audience he hoped there will be a growing number of children who will look up to their parents as people standing up for the world's great cause — Jesus Christ. There is a steady increase, he said, in the number of figures in the professional as well as the amateur sports world who are willing to witness for Christ, willing to stand up and be counted as Christians.

About his conversion as a junior in high school, Glass said, "At first I tried to be like Christians, but that didn't satisfy me, I had to be a Christian myself. We must have Christ within us, recognize our sinfulness and his power to forgive us and to save us. Christ not only forgives us but he motivates us. He gives us something to live for."

Among those in the crusade audience hearing the big Texan give his Christian testimony were Mrs. Graham and sons, Franklin and Ned, and the Graham family maid of 15 years, Beatrice Long. It was the first time Mrs. Long had ever attended a crusade service although she had seen the evangelist preach on television.

On the platform were groups of clergymen from Memphis, Tenn., and Macon, Ga., who had come to invite Billy to conduct crusades in their cities. The following night delegations came from seven other cities.

Hearing Glass and the Graham sermon were groups from several schools who sat in bodies. They included Greenville and Wade Hampton high schools. A teacher who accompanied stu-

dents to several services said, "These young people have found
something they've been looking for. I've never seen such a
change around the school. They are genuinely interested in the
messages and what Dr. Graham is saying to them is being
taken very seriously. When these big, older boys begin carry-
ing their Bibles around in public places, that's a good sign."

Miss Bonnie Barrows, now a student at Wheaton College,
was a senior and president of the student body at Wade Hampton High School and a shining light among young people during
the Crusade. The eldest daughter of Cliff and Mrs. Barrows,
she served as a counselor for girls and was at the heart of the
crusade. She tells here of the spiritual adventure the crusade
brought to many young people:

"The first big teen-night came on Monday when Steve Sloan
gave his testimony. To many of our high school football players
this was a good excuse to attend the crusade without being
branded as a 'religious guy.' And many did attend. As the
choir rehearsed some friends and I looked around in the audience
to determine where they were sitting. Throughout the sermon
we prayed that the message would find receptive ears and hearts.
Our prayers were answered. Young people by the hundreds
walked forward when Dr. Graham gave the invitation. A star
football player went forth, another, then another. We could
hardly believe our eyes. These were memorable, priceless
moments.

"Back at school nearly everyone began talking about religion, God and faith. The atmosphere was electrifying as athletes,
sorority members, youth leaders told how God had touched
their lives at the crusade. In classrooms religion was discussed
and sometimes there were heated arguments and debates. As
one girl put it, 'Never has there been so much talk about God
around here. It has stimulated the thinking of many kids.'

"With some it was a transformation, with others a reformation.

"One youth who barely ever spoke to me, a miserable boy
who had a 'far-out' philosophy akin to atheism, a beatnik type
who had been running with a wild drinking gang, turned up
one night at the crusade and came up to me with the biggest
smile on his face. I knew something had happened. I had not
had enough faith even to put him on my crusade prayer list.

When he pulled me over he began talking about a wonderful experience with Christ that he had had. I was amazed.

"Next day at school he had a Bible on top of his textbooks — and he wasn't ashamed to tell about it. His first mission field was the smoking shelter at school where his old buddies hung out. They couldn't believe the change that had come over him. He urged them to attend the crusade, and some went. Skeptics predicted, 'He won't hold out two weeks.' But he did! This was a real transformation.

"With others it was slower — a reformation — like the case of the girl who prided herself on being a 'no-God' person. She came one night to the crusade for laughs and later declared that it was all a big farce, an emotional racket. She came, however, a second time, and a third, and before it was over she had a struggle with God. As she related it, she even tried to sit through one service concentrating on 'controlling her emotions.' She gripped her seat and told herself, 'No, no, no.' Yet on the last night she gave up and submitted herself to Christ. She now found forgiveness, and peace and contentment she had never before known.

"The change in attitudes, change in desires, change in people did not end at Textile Hall. Some of the most exciting things were to follow.

"The week after the crusade a group of teenagers, most of them converted at the meetings, met together for fellowship and to share the wonderful experiences that had come into their lives. Many of them had not been church-goers, so the idea of prayer, of faith, and of Christianity as a whole was relatively new to them.

"Conversations sounded like this: 'Before I accepted Christ I had a long list of doubts and excuses. Now that I've become a Christian, I can't even remember what they were.' 'I asked God to help so many people come to know Him that I was sure God could never remember them all.' 'Peanuts is always saying 'Happiness is a warm blanket,' but I have found that happiness is God.'

"Being with Christians — new ones — was refreshing to us older converts. Our lives were changed by their enthusiasm and desire to know God intimately. We who had lived with our spiritual heirlooms began dusting them off to see if they were real and truly ours.

"One get-together led to another. We had real Bible studies, felt free to express opinions, share our problems, ask questions — but our Christian advisor always led us back to God's word for the final answer.

"Young people were saved even during the fellowship meetings. One girl who had walked out of a crusade service, rejecting God's Spirit moving in her heart, was finally brought to Christ. She believed that she had turned her back and had lost her last chance to receive Him. But she was wrong. God led her to our Bible study group the night we watched a crusade telecast. She heard again the sermon she walked out on and with tears streaming down her face she told the thirty-five teenagers in that room, 'Christ has come in tonight. I'm so thankful He didn't give up on me.'

"We met together, we prayed, we shared — and never before had we known such wonderful friends. God is continuing to work — and we stand in amazement, thrilled beyond words at what He is doing. We cannot help but say, 'How Great Thou Art'."

Many who went forward at the crusade were not even teenagers. The Rev. James Covington, pastor of Aldersgate Methodist Church, wrote this in his church letter:

> At our evening worship service Sunday we had a period of sharing testimonials and spiritual victories that happened as a result of the Billy Graham Crusade. One testimony that seemed to have meant so much to everyone was expressed by an eight-year-old boy who stood up, almost unnoticed, and told that he had accepted Jesus Christ as his own Saviour during the Crusade. If this Crusade has done anything, it has certainly made me realize more than ever before that these young children know what they are doing and they know what they want as far as their response to Jesus Christ is concerned. I think this was evidenced by the fact that of the 64 who responded from our church, all but 15 were between the ages of seven and seventeen. Certainly the words of Isaiah are true here when he says, 'And a little child shall lead them.'

John Lenning of Greenville, a crusade associate, served as advisor to a group of young people who decided for God at the crusade and wanted to continue meeting together for fellow-ship. "As the days go by we continue to hear of lives that were changed during the crusade," he said. "I have had the privilege of meeting with a group of teenagers each week. Most of the group, which numbers around twenty, made decisions at the crusade. Five or six made first-time commitments to Christ. It is a real thrill to see these young people gain new victories in Christ day by day. A few days ago I talked to a housewife who told me that the crusade had brought a real change in their family even though each member of their family had accepted Christ before the crusade. One day, when we are with Christ, these stories and many others will be known in full by all of us who had the opportunity to invest a part of our lives in the Billy Graham Southern Piedmont Crusade."

Two-thirds of the 7,311 crusade inquirers were under age 19 and 2,194 of them (30 per cent of the total) were in the 15-18 category.

The following statistical report covers only those who went forward in Textile Hall during the crusade and does not reflect the several hundreds who called by telephone on the nights of the crusade television programs or the thousands who made decisions during the showing of "The Restless Ones" in Green-ville, Spartanburg, and Anderson the weeks following the crusade.

Here is the summary report on crusade inquirers:

### Age Categories

| TOTAL | 5-11 | 12-14 | 15-18 | 19-29 | 30-49 | 50+ | UN-KNOWN |
|-------|------|-------|-------|-------|-------|-----|----------|
| 7,311 | 901 | 1,802 | 2,194 | 1,216 | 797 | 260 | 141 |
| 100% | 12.3 | 24.6 | 30.0 | 16.6 | 10.9 | 3.5 | 1.9 |

### Type of Decision

| ACCEPT | DEDI-CATION | ASSUR-ANCE | RESTO-RATION | OTHER | TOTAL |
|--------|-------------|------------|--------------|-------|-------|
| 2,477 | 2,688 | 753 | 1,353 | 40 | 7,311 |
| 33.6% | 36.7 | 10.2 | 18.5 | .5 | |

(The category identified as "Accept" indicates a first-time commitment to Christ. The inquirer listed in the "Dedication" column makes a definite act of dedication of his life for Christian service, having already received Christ. The category identified as "Assurance" means that the inquirer is concerned with his relationship with God and although he may be trusting Christ for salvation lacks a basic assurance and is simply inquiring as to his specific relationship with God. The "Restoration" category indicates the inquirer who previously received Christ as Saviour but for some reason stopped walking in fellowship with God and is now, under the conviction of the Holy Spirit, coming back to God to be restored to fellowship with Him).

# 12

The relationship of the Billy Graham Evangelistic Association with seminaries and seminary students across America is an aspect of crusade influence that has been relatively unknown, even to the masses of people attending Graham services.

In a special orientation and training program for seminary students, developed in recent years, selected young men from a number of seminaries of various denominations are brought in to have a first-hand involvement in crusade evangelism. The seminarians participate in group discussions, observe the total crusade organization, participate in seminars with Graham team members, take counselor training and actually serve in the meetings as counselors.

The program in Greenville was conducted under the general supervision of Crusade Director Forrest Layman, with the Rev. William L. Palmer of Greenville as coordinator.

"Only eternity will reveal the inestimable value of the program," said Mr. Palmer, who is pastor of Edwards Road Baptist Church. "In consideration of the far-reaching influence through the challenged and changed lives of seminary students the program is one of the outstanding features of the campaign."

The sixty-three seminarians who participated in the Greenville Crusade came from fourteen seminaries and graduate

schools of religion throughout the United States.[1] Expenses
for their transportation, room and board were paid by an anony-
mous Texas benefactor.

The orientation program dates were March 2-9, with a rather
heavy schedule daily, and the men lived at the Jack Tar Poinsett Hotel. The plan was designed to instill vision in the students
for increased ministry in evangelism and the crusade provided
the opportunity for them to observe the Graham team in action,
to receive training for evangelism and to gain practical experience in counseling. Students from widely divergent theological
backgrounds were able to interact and evaluate mass evangelism
from their own perspective.

"They readily expressed differing personal convictions which
would have placed them in any number of categories from ultra-
fundamentalist to ultra-radical," Mr. Palmer reported. "There
were Negro and white students and the group included Canadi-
ans, a German, a Dutchman, a Brazilian and a Spaniard.

"Upon their arrival at the hotel, where all stayed and where
classes were held for one week, the men were evidently both
eager and hesitant, cooperative and antagonistic. Their lives
and attitudes and concepts were being challenged. Some were
changed. The initial touch-and-go and stab-and-retreat developed into some most constructive give-and-take and mutual
enlightening of understanding. The rapport which evolved
through post-crusade discussion periods was unbelievably good.
A religion reporter described one of the bull sessions with
these young theologians as the most informative religious gathering in which he had been an observer in 20 years.

"The seminarians had personal contact with the team mem-

[1]The students came from the following schools: Asbury Theological
Seminary, Wilmore, Ky.; Candler School of Theology at Emory Uni-
versity, Atlanta, Ga.; Columbia Theological Seminary, Decatur, Ga.;
Covenant Theological Seminary, St. Louis, Mo.; Dallas Theological
Seminary, Dallas, Texas; Fuller Theological Seminary, Pasadena,
Calif.; Hood Theological Seminary, Salisbury, N. C.; Lutheran Theo-
logical Southern Seminary, Columbia, S. C.; School of Theology, The
University of the South, Sewanee, Tenn.; Simmons University, Louis-
ville, Ky.; Southern Baptist Theological Seminary, Louisville, Ky.;
J. J. Starks Center of Training, Benedict College, Columbia, S. C.;
Union Theological Seminary, Richmond, Va.; Wheaton Graduate
School, Wheaton, Ill.

bers. They came to know them as real men and spiritual leaders of capability, conviction and concern. Ten of the men sat on the platform each night during the week of the orientation program. There and in the classes they came into personal contact with the outstanding laymen who were involved in the crusade activities. The seminarians were influenced as they came to know something of the heartbeat and desire of the laymen in their concern for revival in Greenville.

"The young men who participated in the Orientation Program in Greenville will never be the same. A significant contribution was made to their ministry. They had an outstanding experience in their theological education. The week was probably one of the best and most profitable that any of them ever spent.

"This program could do more through seminary students to influence the future of church attitudes toward evangelism than almost any other emphasis of the Billy Graham Evangelistic Association."

Greenville area ministers and laymen working on crusade committees who met with the students were from many denominations including Baptist, Presbyterian, Episcopal, Methodist, Pentecostal. Members of the Graham organization instructed the students in every aspect of Crusade from music to magazines. The Graham organization included Akbar Abdul-Haqq, Cliff Barrows, Leighton Ford, Ray Harvey, Don Hustad, Forrest Layman, Walter Smyth, Grady Wilson, Sherwood Wirt. The pastors were Cullen Crook, Welcome Baptist Church, Greenville; Newman Faulconer, First Presbyterian Church, Greenville; Clyde Ireland, Rector, the Church of the Redeemer Episcopal, Greenville; L. D. Johnson, First Baptist Church, Greenville; William L. Palmer, Edwards Road Baptist Church, Greenville; Calvin Thielman, Presbyterian Church, Montreat, N. C. Laymen appearing before the group were Jim Orders, Methodist; Harrison Rearden, Baptist; Max Rice, Baptist; Jack Shaw, Pentecostal; Col. C. E. Singleton, Baptist; Murray Woodward, Baptist.

The students joined with ministers from throughout the Piedmont area for the pre-crusade meeting addressed by Billy Graham at the Greenville Baptist Church.

For many of the seminarians the crusade and its related program for them became a treasured experience and memory.

Some who had taken a dim view of mass evangelism now saw immense spiritual values in the Graham crusade method. The crusade impact on the students was indicated in critiques and letters they sent to Mr. Palmer.

Wrote one: "I shall remember, with gratitude, the time spent there in learning and growing. Many profitable things were gained, not the least of which is a renewed appreciation of God's response to prayer and the exciting way He draws men to Himself."

Here is an excerpt from another's letter: "It is hard for us to express properly our appreciation for the days we spent in Greenville. We are fully persuaded that the value to us cannot be measured. In a very definite way I have felt led of the Lord into some type of education and evangelistic work."

Another wrote: "The Orientation Program was a great success and something which I will not lightly forget. It was a time in which God spoke to me and caused me to reevaluate many of my concepts of evangelism, both mass evangelism and personal evangelism."

One who indicated soon after arriving in Greenville that he intended to do no more than stand on the sideline and look with indifference because he held strong theological differences with Billy Graham came to a most unexpected experience at the crusade. He wrote Mr. Palmer a month later of the change that had come in his thinking and in his life. "Something told me that I had to go forward when Billy gave the invitation at the first service on Wednesday night. So I did, and I thank God for Billy Graham." He added: "The orientation program put a new dimension in my theological education and in my life."

"To be there was a thrilling and invaluable experience," a student said in his letter. "As I sat on the platform that first night both singing and listening to the words of 'All Hail the Power of Jesus Name', I knew that the Holy Spirit was in our midst, and as I looked out on the throng of people, row after row, I realized that those faces stretched back two thousand years. I thrilled as I caught a new glimpse of the power of His name."

Here are excerpts from other letters:

"I am a more useful instrument for God today than before I came to the crusade."

"I may forget many of the things I have learned in seminary training, but I will never forget this opportunity to see God at work in the lives of men and to feel this work in my own life."

"My ministry will always show favorably many insights that I gained in Greenville during the Billy Graham Crusade."

"It was one of the greatest weeks of my life."

"My faith for the ministry has been strengthened."

The relationship of Billy Graham and the crusade with the general public as well as the news media was handled by Gil Stricklin, a newspaper man turned preacher, and public relations member of the organization. The extra-crusade engagements Billy Graham filled had been scheduled weeks ahead and he could not accept any of the scores of invitations to speak and make personal appearances that came during the crusade. It would take over one hundred years to fill all the invitations he received, Gil Stricklin estimated. On one day invitations to hold crusades or rallies were extended by seven cities.

Mr. Stricklin worked behind the scenes to aid the press, television and radio in crusade coverage. His crusade day started early in the morning and continued until long after the final evening services. His phone often began ringing before 7:00 A.M. One day, a count showed, he received 78 incoming calls at his crusade information office.

Some calls were from people outside the news reporting field asking to see Billy Graham or to obtain his autograph. One caller wanted Billy to visit his ill daughter in a hospital and to pray for her. Many requests involved special problems and Mr. Stricklin sought to be helpful in each instance.

In the case of the father with the stricken daughter, Mr. Stricklin explained that the evangelist's strength and schedule would not allow a hospital visit at the time. On the telephone, Mr. Stricklin prayed for the ill child and for the parents, and the caller expressed his gratitude to him.

On the last Sunday of the crusade Billy said that he had turned down at least 100 social invitations during the ten days and expressed regret that he did not get to know more people personally. But, he promised, "When we get to heaven, I'll come over to your home on 'Forgiveness Avenue' and sip tea with you for a hundred years." The audience smiled approvingly.

In his apologies he noted that in addition to being unable to have personal contact with many people, his children "had to get an appointment to see me." He added, "They must wonder what kind of daddy I am." (When Mrs. Graham drove down from Montreat with the Graham children to attend a crusade service Anne asked, "Can I see Daddy and tell him I love him?" He was in meditation and study at his motel quarters, but Associate Evangelist T. W. Wilson, who handles Graham appointments, took her forthwith to see him.)

Billy Graham's only speech outside of Textile Hall during the crusade came March 8 at a breakfast meeting of the Greenville Chamber of Commerce Buttonhole Club. He told the record audience of 500 that America's moral crisis "will ultimately determine the future of this nation." Calling "total license" and "total control of offspring" products of the same materialistic view of man and the same secularistic view of life and society," the evangelist warned that "whichever one wins, 'the American way of life' is doomed."

America can't survive its crisis of moral decline unless the people decide on "a great spiritual awakening," he declared.

Referring to "vast programs to feed and develop our bodies," he pointed to the lack of programs to "develop the moral and spiritual side of man" as "what's missing from the 'great society' today." "Our generation has been" living like parasites on the spiritual capital of our predecessors. But he predicted confidently that a return to the Christian concepts and beliefs of our forefathers and rededication to Jesus Christ "would change the moral tone of the nation . . . strengthen our home life . . . put sex in the right perspective . . . give purpose to young people . . . restore a high sense of destiny to our nation."

The meeting, largest in the club's eleven-year history, was presided over by Norvin Duncan. The evangelist was introduced by Dr. L. D. Johnson, who said "Billy Graham has been given by God the gift of being a prophet."

# 13

D<small>URING</small> <small>THE DAYS OF THE CRUSADE, TRAFFIC TO</small> T<small>EXTILE</small> H<small>ALL WAS</small>
very heavy and slow-moving. Traffic-jammed motorists were
understanding, however, and visibly more patient and relaxed.
One driver who had to wait for about twenty minutes was seen
sitting singing the powerful hymns of the revival. Billy Graham
heard about it and told his audience, "Revival has come if we
can be patient in a traffic jam."

A small incident in the thick of crusade traffic stands out
in the mind of Dr. Wallace Fridy, Anderson co-chairman of the
crusade. As he drove to the second service on Friday night
when attendance hit 36,000, a busy but tired traffic policeman,
noticing the "Crusade Official" and clergy identification on the
car creeping past, said to Dr. Fridy, "Pray for me." The policeman was in good spirits and smiling in spite of his fatigue, Dr.
Fridy said.

At the service Dr. Fridy sat on the platform next to Dr. James
S. Day, the Spartanburg co-chairman. Taking in the scene of
the packed hall with an embracing glance, Dr. Day commented,
"I have never seen as much prayer and publicity as in this
crusade."

Nodding in agreement, Dr. Fridy replied, "And to these two
we could add good preaching. In fact, I guess we would list
prayer, preaching, publicity, parking and if singing started with

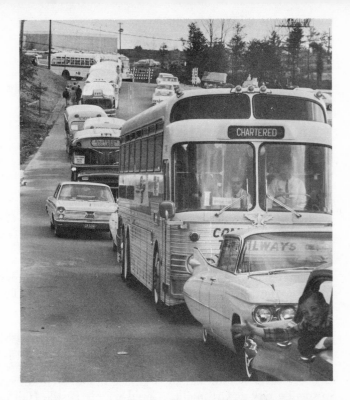

Busses and crowds (News-Piedmont photos)

a 'p' we could list it too. I have never seen such news coverage as has been given in this crusade."

Weeks after the final service Dr. Day viewed the crusade in retrospect and noted his observations as follows:

"Would the Gospel-hardened Piedmont Bible Belt respond to the evangelistic appeal and the twentieth-century revival methods of Billy Graham and his team? These and other questions kept returning to my mind after I had accepted the crusade chairmanship for the Spartanburg area.

"I knew, of course, how God had blessed Dr. Graham's evangelistic ministry in the far West and in the North. In many of these areas, however, old-fashioned revival meetings and crusades were 'so old' that they were 'novel and new' to thousands of nominal church members and completely unheard of by thousands of non-church members. Would the Piedmont respond to Billy Graham as it had to Billy Sunday in Spartanburg way back in the bitter cold winter of 1921, when they ran excursion trains and had to have three services on the closing Sunday?

"But the Billy Sunday Tabernacle in Spartanburg seated only 5,000. The new Textile Hall in Greenville seated over 20,000. Never before had so large a crusade been attempted in so small a city as Greenville. Could we fill Textile Hall even on the closing Sunday? I remembered that the Coliseum in Charlotte (Dr. Graham's 'home town' and a much larger city than Greenville) seated only 16,000.

"Another question kept pressing for an answer. Would the 'liturgical' pastors, many of whom had not had a revival in their own churches in many years, respond and cooperate with Dr. Graham? At the other end of the 'theological rainbow,' would the ultra-fundamental and conservative churches and pastors cooperate?

"Then there was the distance problem. It had been agreed from the beginning that only with the active assistance of Spartanburg and Anderson could Greenville undertake so large a crusade. But these cities were miles away from Greenville and had their own city and county loyalties. One evangelistic pastor said to me: 'Day, I can't get many of my own members to attend revival services in our own church. How can I get them to attend a crusade thirty-one miles away?' The Graham team had never before attempted a crusade on a three-county or a three-city basis. Would they consider it just a Greenville crusade or in reality the Southern Piedmont Crusade?

"Then I remembered the problem of finances. In my fourteen and a half years as a pastor in Spartanburg I had seen and been active in a number of city and area revivals. Because of spiritual indifference, many of these revivals had to major on getting cash instead of getting converts in their closing services. This concern was felt by many when the Executive Committee considered the preliminary budget, which seemed huge. This concern deepened as the time for the crusade approached, and our large advance gifts, especially in Spartanburg and Anderson, continued to lag. This concern increased almost to alarm when we found that we had to enlarge the budget by about $20,000 just a few weeks before the crusade opening. Had we gone overboard in our budget plans?

"I was mindful also that, human nature being what it is, we would have to answer the question (sometimes spoken and always implied): 'What will my church get out of the crusade? How many new members will my church receive?'

"But, thanks be to God, all of these fears and doubts were groundless. Elsewhere the details of the remarkable Billy Graham Southern Piedmont Crusade are given, including attendance, number of decisions and finances. The results are now history. To God be the glory!

"In my own church we received sixty new members. This includes the periods before and after the crusade. Most of these came as a result of the crusade, directly or indirectly. And they are still coming as we feel the spiritual impact of the film, 'The Restless Ones,' shown two months after the crusade itself ended.

"Yes, I am 'sold' on Billy Graham, his team and his methods. I believe he is God's man for this hour."

Spartanburg Night at the crusade was Wednesday, the first night of double services. Dr. Day gave the offertory prayer and Spartanburg's Mayor Robert L. Stoddard sat on the platform as special guest.

Before the 35,000 who heard him at the two services, Billy said that heaven "is not going to be a place where we sit under palm trees and listen to beautiful music. It is going to be labor, adventure, excitement, employment and engagement. Heaven will be the picture we have always longed for. It will be the new social order that men have dreamed of. All the things that made earth unlovely and tragic will be absent in heaven. There will be no night, no death, no disease, no sorrow, no tears, no ignorance, no disappointments, no war. It will be filled with health, vigor, knowledge, happiness, love and perfection."

Speaking from a flower-decked rostrum, flanked by the 2,500 voice choir, the evangelist said heaven has been described as "a new creation in which we will move in a new body, possess a new name, sing new songs, live in a new city governed by a new form of government and challenged by new prospects of eternity."

Billy said one of man's oldest questions is, is there life after death? The Bible's answer is yes, he added, and Christ is the great authority on the question because he was raised from the dead.

Jesus also taught of hell, he continued. "The very essence of hell is separation from God. Hell is associated with fire, darkness and death. Fire can create a thirst. This could be a thirst for God. Darkness is the absence of light. God is the source of eternal life and darkness is the result of God's absence. Death is also an absence of life, and God is the source of all eternal life."

The crusade on this night brought together two Negro singers — Ethel Waters, whose international fame had been established over the past half century on a rich voice and glowing personality, and 19-year-old Myrtle Hall, on the threshold of a promising musical career, appearing for the first time before a large audience.

Miss Hall, who has studied music most of her life, sang her first real solo with the Greenville Symphony Orchestra when she was 11. Several Greenville residents became convinced she might win a scholarship to Juilliard. She did, in an audition in September, 1964.

Miss Hall arrived in Greenville just in time for the first service that evening. She was smiling and appeared confident, concealing her stage fright, when she approached the lectern to sing after Cliff Barrows introduced her with a prediction that she would be heard for many years to come. He had heard her at Christmastime 1964, in Greenville's Memorial Auditorium, where both participated in a community sing event, and, he said, "she has been a blessing wherever she has sung." The hymn she chose has been a favorite for generations — "Stranger of Galilee —" and her lyric soprano voice rang clearly through the building as she sang at both services.

"That was wonderful," Billy Graham whispered to her after she sat down following her song at the early service.

Between services Miss Waters arrived to be a platform guest after having sung at all services for the four previous nights. Her face beaming, she embraced Miss Hall with warmth and affection for a younger singer of potential greatness. Later, after hearing her sing, Miss Waters exclaimed, "I think she is wonderful! God has given her a voice that has beauty and a wholesome quality."

The team members were impressed by Miss Hall's singing, and that evening invited her to go to London in June to sing in the crusade at Earls Court. When she appeared in the London Crusade as one of the evangelist's soloists she was loudly applauded by the large audiences.

"I have never been so frightened in my life as when I stepped up to sing at the crusade in Textile Hall," Miss Hall said the next day at a committee meeting of the Zonta Club of Greenville. "I have always been able to see the audience before, but there I couldn't tell where the audience began and where it ended. It was all around. I was overwhelmed with the large crowd."

# 14

Billy Graham came to Greenville after nineteen years of crusades in more than thirty nations, attended by fifty million people. He and his team received a warm and enthusiastic welcome.

In an official greeting, Mayor David G. Traxler wrote: "We have waited a long time for the crusade and your visit and we are thankful that the hour has now come. This great religious undertaking will be a rich and meaningful experience for our entire area." When the evangelist spoke at a breakfast in Greenville a year earlier Mayor Traxler presented Billy a printed certificate making him an honorary citizen of the city. In like manner Mayor Robert L. Stoddard conferred an honorary citizenship of Spartanburg on him.

At forty-eight one of the world's best known figures, Billy has counseled and shared gospel messages with presidents and crowned heads, elite and commoners, wealthy and poor around the globe. As a teenager his faith led him to the foot of the cross and his devotion to God and unshakable faith have brought him to the place he occupies today as perhaps the most effective and influential evangelist of modern times.

He says there are thousands of better preachers than he and that he is only a willing instrument for the spreading of the Gospel. Wherever he has gone around the world, however, ministers of various faiths testify to the unusual power and

Dr. Graham shares songbook with Mayor Robert L.
Stoddard of Spartanburg, South Carolina.

Mayor John W. Glenn of Anderson (center) was Dr. Graham's
platform companion on "Anderson" night . Dr. Wallace  Fridy,
pastor of St. John's Methodist Church, Anderson, who read
Scripture is next right (News-Piedmont photos)

unique blessings experienced by those who attend the services. The true symbol of his success lies in the changed lives of people who have heard him.

The six members who made up the Graham organization in the previous South Carolina crusade — at Columbia in the spring of 1950 — were in Greenville sixteen years later as key figures in the Southern Piedmont Crusade. They were Billy Graham, Cliff Barrows, Grady Wilson, George Beverly Shea, Tedd Smith and Willis Haymaker.

Other team members serving in the Greenville Crusade included Forrest Layman, Walter H. Smith, Leighton Ford, Howard O. Jones, Dr. Akbar Abdul Haqq, Dr. T. W. Wilson, Jr., Don Hustad, and George Wilson. Others of the Graham organization who had important roles in the Crusade were Dr. Sherwood Wirt, John Lenning, Gil Stricklin, Hank Beukema.

Cliff Barrows, the Number Two man next to Billy Graham, on the most potent evangelistic team of the century, is more than a person. He is an institution. As music, radio and television director of the Billy Graham Evangelistic Association (BGEA), he has become the most famous musical evangelist since the Homer Rodeheaver era. His latest venture is into film-making, and he has been made president of World Wide Pictures, a BGEA subsidary which produced "For Pete's Sake," "The Restless Ones," and other releases.

One of the first things observers often comment about in a Graham crusade is the finesse of the volunteer choir. It takes more than musical ability and pleasing personality to build a crusade choir such as sang in Greenville. Although Cliff Barrows has these qualities, he has more. God has given him the confidence of singers and would-be singers in nations around the world. On the final day of the crusade, Cliff received long and loud applause from his home city audience.

"If you asked me who was the greatest Christian I know, it'd be a toss-up between Cliff and my wife," Billy Graham said.

"He is greatly admired for his ability to direct great choirs, and for the wonderful work he is doing, but I admire him even more for his ability to radiate love for God," said Mrs. Katherine Johnson, a counselor and member of the Greenville choir. "In all he does, directing, talking, in his prayers, his life shines radiantly. It is as though he had a fountain of deep devotion for God, always bubbling up and running over."

More than a choir leader and radio producer, Cliff has the responsibility for directing the entire service from the platform until the moment Billy begins his message. And even then Cliff holds Billy's microphone wire so that the evangelist has complete freedom of moving, as he preaches, without danger of becoming entangled with the cord.

When at home with his family in Greenville, Cliff spends much time working on the recorded tapes for the "Hour of Decision" program and for "Prayer Time" tapes which are played over local radio stations just prior to each crusade. John Lenning puts the tapes together.

Cliff and Billy have been working together for the Lord since 1945 when Cliff and his wife, Billie, were on their honeymoon and attended a Youth for Christ rally in Asheville, N. C. Billy Graham was the speaker and when the scheduled song leader failed to show up, Cliff was "drafted" to substitute. The team was there formed and the rest is history.

Since 1947 Cliff and Bev Shea have been the musical nucleus of both the Billy Graham Crusade services and the Hour of Decision radio programs.

"There is no substitute for sacred music in preparing the hearts of the people for the spoken word," says Mr. Shea, who lives in Western Springs, Ill., with his wife and their two children.

"If your song is to reach hearts, of course it must come from your heart," he said.

Bev Shea's warm baritone voice is always heard just before the evangelist's sermon. He feels that the hymns sung in a Christian worship service should not be regarded merely as preliminaries, but as an integral part of the service. His recordings and radio appearances as well as his work with the Billy Graham team have made his voice familiar to millions in many lands.

The son of a Methodist minister, Mr. Shea once was an insurance executive in New York. Later he was announcer and staff soloist for Station WMBI, Chicago. He composed the music for "I'd Rather Have Jesus," one of his best-known solos. Other songs he has written include "The Wonder of It All," "Sing Me a Song of Sharon's Rose" and "I Love Thy Presence, Lord."

"Bev" Shea

Cliff Barrows at rehearsal  (News-Piedmont photo)

Grady Wilson

George Wilson

T. W. Wilson

Two of the three Wilsons on the Graham team are brothers — Drs. Grady Wilson and T. W., Jr. The third Wilson, George, is not related to them.

George Wilson and his family live in Minneapolis. Since 1950 he has been an executive with the Graham organization. Known for his keen business sense, he serves as executive vice president and treasurer of the Billy Graham Evangelistic Association. "When George makes a recommendation Billy usually goes along with it," a person close to the team said.

Grady and T. W. Wilson and Billy Graham were boyhood friends in their native Charlotte, N. C. Grady and Billy were roommates at Wheaton College, where both graduated. After a few years as pastor at Moncks Corner, and then Charleston, S. C., Grady entered evangelistic work full time and joined Billy Graham in 1947 as his associate. With Cliff Barrows and Bev Shea they formed a team of four to hold meetings on a city-wide basis.

Grady, his wife and their two daughters make their home in Charlotte. His devotion to God's Word and his desire to be spent in the divine task of making Christ known have kept Grady faithful to his post regardless of where the work of the Graham organization takes him. He is well known for his infectious jovial manner, quick wit and ability to entertain with illimitable stories, humorous experiences and impersonations. He is a gifted speaker and his familiar voice reading Scripture has been heard by millions since the inauguration of the "Hour of Decision" radio broadcast in 1950. He has led many revivals. Following the 1966 London crusade, he went to Harlan, Ky., and conducted a week-long meeting in a park of that coal mining community.

T. W. Wilson, a former Baptist preacher, has had the title of associate evangelist on the Billy Graham team since 1956. He is one of the closest persons to Billy Graham, was vice president of Northwestern Schools in Minneapolis (1948-51) when Billy was its president.

The Wilson family live at Montreat, about a mile down the mountain from the Grahams. He handles Billy's appointments and is his traveling companion. Together they have traveled throughout the world, in every direction on the compass and back again, and have logged enough flying hours to qualify as airline pilots. Their travels have taken them into the presence of kings and queens, as well as presidents and governors and famous people of many lands.

Tedd Smith, universally recognized as one of the outstanding pianists in the field of religious music, joined Billy Graham in Columbia, S. C., in the spring of 1950 and has been playing in Graham crusades and rallies since. He is a recording artist and has written several piano hymn arrangements books, including *Crusade Piano Solos, Nos. 1 and 2*, published by Zondervan. Tedd and his family live in Silver Spring, Md.

At the organ for each service was Dr. Donald P. Hustad, a concert artist, composer and lecturer, who for fifteen years was director of the Department of Sacred Music at Moody Bible Institute, Chicago. As Graham team organist, his music has set the spiritual tone of hundreds of meetings and awakened longings in many hearts. He will continue with the Graham organization until 1967, when he becomes professor of church music at Southern Baptist Theological Seminary, Louisville, Ky.

Leighton Ford, a Canadian-born Presbyterian preacher, has conducted crusades of his own, mostly in Canada. He joined the Graham team in 1955 and has substituted in the pulpit a number of times when Billy Graham has been ill. He is married to Billy's sister, the former Jean Coffey Graham, and they and their three children live in Charlotte, N. C. He is the author of a book on evangelism.

Walter H. Smyth, a vice president of BGEA, is responsible for the direction of team activities and the planning and organization of all the crusades. He handles personnel assignments in connection with the team office and crusade preparation. It is sometimes necessary to prepare for several crusades at one time. He and his family live in Atlanta, where he opened a team office in 1964.

Forrest Layman played a major role in the preparations for the crusade in Greenville. As director, he was at the heart of crusade planning and activity. He and John Lenning were chiefly responsible for the splendid counselor training and follow-up programs, the crusade office, and other activities. An articulate speaker and Bible scholar, Mr. Layman is executive

Don Hustad at the console of the organ (News-Piedmont photo)

assistant for team activities and crusade planning in the Atlanta office.

The Rev. Howard O. Jones has been an associate evangelist with the team since 1958, spending about half his time in Africa and half in the United States. While serving as pastor of Smoot Memorial Church in Cleveland, Ohio, he developed an African radio ministry with station ELWA, Monrovia, Liberia. He is author of a book, *Shall We Overcome?* and his "Hour of Freedom" radio program is being aired from several American cities. A native of Cleveland, he was a dance band saxophonist prior to his conversion.

W. Stanley Mooneyham, special assistant to Billy Graham, advised and aided in early preparations for the crusade before moving from Atlanta with his family to Berlin, Germany, early in 1966 to open an office and serve as coordinating director of the World Congress on Evangelism in the famed Kongresshalle October 26 – November 4.

Willis Haymaker, associate crusade director, came to Greenville weeks in advance of the crusade and had charge of the organization of prayer groups, and assisted with other phases of crusade planning. When Billy Graham was a small boy Mr. Haymaker was a friend of the Graham family. In the 1930's he was associated with Gypsy Smith, the English evangelist, making advance arrangements for Smith's preaching missions in the United States. Since 1950 Mr. Haymaker has been connected with the Graham organization.

Night after night, without let up, crowds poured into Textile Hall in unexpectedly large numbers to hear the dynamic Graham preaching and soul-stirring music of the Crusade. Escalation of the crusade at the midway point resulted in an audience of 16,000 at the first service on Wednesday night and 19,000 at the second. That night he brought his listeners face to face with the prospect of death and promised there would be immortality through faith in Jesus Christ.

Attendance at the two services was 36,600 on Thursday, 28,000 on Friday and 36,300 on Saturday. Billy's vibrant voice showed no sign of weakening. "I never have any trouble with my voice," he said earlier in the week, and the course of the crusade was bearing him out.

Near the end of the crusade, J. Hunter Stokes, *Greenville News* assistant city editor, wrote this about the evangelist:

> Dr. Graham's stamina seems unflagging. If anything, he has been more vigorous at the second services of the past two days. Only on Wednesday did he seem to tire as the night wore on. Exercise has helped him — he played golf yesterday for the fourth time since he has been here — and he eats "at least four good meals a day." He also has the ability to relax completely in little time and even manages to sleep during the hour between services. He will greet just a few people, shower and rest between appearances.

Dr. Cort R. Flint, Anderson Baptist minister who has known Billy Graham for a number of years, gave this description of the evangelist's preparation and preaching:

> Two hours before Mr. Graham is to preach, he cuts himself off from everyone to pray and prepare his heart and mind for God's message to the people. Even though he may repeat some of the same statements that he has made thousands of times, he must have the anointing and infilling of God's Spirit to speak to the people.
>
> The deep compassion for every person to know Christ is always upon him, but in these two hours before he preaches, there is the agony of suffering and longing for their souls. It is during this period that he identifies closely with Christ in the Garden of Gethsemane so that the will of God in the redemption of mankind can take place. He feels the heavy burden that all who listen shall be transformed and drawn near to the heart of God. In this aspect of his life he is praying for the world as John Knox did when he said, "Give me souls or I die." Knox prayed with such fervor and faith that the Queen of the Scots trembled in fear of this man of God.
>
> In this intercessory prayer for those who will listen to his voice Mr. Graham comes close to death as he experiences the pain, the despair, the desperation and the terrible lostness of man without God. His body perspires, his breathing becomes difficult and his heart beats rapidly as he lays himself prostrate before God.
>
> As he comes from his room to the place where he is to preach, he has to go through the rush of seeing the groups who want him to conduct revivals in their city, the special requests of people connected with the crusade, the friends who have come from distant places to be with him again and the dignitaries who are to be on the platform. He moves through these with ease, but it takes a toll upon his strength and interferes

James B. Orders, Jr., Crusade Co-chairman (Joe Jordan photo);
Dr. Wallace Fridy; Dr. James S. Day, Jr., Crusade Co-chairman.

with the spiritual power that has been building up within him. He then goes to the platform where the members of the team see that he is left alone for the final impartation of God's Spirit upon him.

The evangelist pours out his heart as he proclaims the Gospel of salvation. Again he goes through the agony, the perspiration, the heartache, the compassion and the complete surrender that God will be speaking through him. He constantly reminds his listeners that there is a second voice of the Holy Spirit giving a personal message according to each individual need and how everyone is to respond.

His gifted oratory under the leadership of God has a deep effect upon all, even the most cynical. Billy Graham is God's prophet for this generation and no one can go away without realizing something of the closeness and nearness of God.

# 15

THE GENERAL ASSEMBLY OF SOUTH CAROLINA TOOK OFFICIAL note of the crusade and adopted a resolution expressing "sincerest gratitude" to Billy Graham and his evangelistic team for bringing a religious revival to the state.

Governor Robert E. McNair, who with Mrs. McNair attended the opening service, was moved to make this comment about the Crusade: "South Carolina was highly honored to have been chosen for Dr. Billy Graham's only crusade in America during 1966. The opportunity to attend the first evening of the Crusade, as a platform guest, was a heart-warming and stimulating experience for me. It was obvious from the reception of the audience that our people have a great hunger for spiritual guidance. I am hopeful that the effects of this evangelistic crusade will be of lasting benefit to our state and all of the many thousands who came to hear Dr. Graham's messages and to worship together."

The legislative resolution noted that:

> 278,700 persons attended the 10-day Crusade and 7,300 men, women and young people responded to Dr. Graham's invitation to the altar to reaffirm their faith and to publicly proclaim repentance for their sins and their determination to mold their lives anew in the pattern of Jesus Christ.

The effects of the Crusade on the people of the area, the churches, the communities and even on future generations are imponderable and immeasurable.

The seeds of spiritual renewal, sown by Dr. Graham and believed to have fallen on fertile ground, have already sprouted and the harvest is expected to reach far beyond the environs of the Piedmont area.

At a great sacrifice to himself, both physically and mentally, Dr. Graham graciously consented to hold two services daily, which was the first time this has ever been done by him in this country.

Authors of the resolution were Reps. Richard W. Riley, Herbert Granger, Rex L. Carter, Fred Fuller, Charlie Garrett, Beattie Huff, Lloyd Hunt, Harry Chapman, Clyde Jenkins, Nick Theodore and Fred McDonald.

The only voiced criticism of the crusade or of Billy Graham came from Bob Jones University. The night before the crusade opened the school's president, Dr. Bob Jones, Jr., went on a local television station and issued a statement to the press attacking the evangelist and his crusade methods. Billy did not reply, following a long-observed policy of ignoring such criticism.

An audit of the crusade books showed cash receipts of $198,146.38, and its cash disbursements included $15,565.92 over costs that went to the Billy Graham Nationwide Television and Radio Ministry. The money over expenses had been designated for that purpose by the Executive Committee at the time a budget was prepared.

Originally budgeted at $167,555 the Crusade expenses were increased when attendance exceeded the seating capacity in Textile Hall and two daily sessions were held the last five days. The added expenditures reflected in part a nearly doubled amount for advertising and publicity for the daily sessions. Advertisements were run in newspapers in Atlanta, Charlotte, Asheville, Columbia, Spartanburg and Anderson, as well as in Greenville.

Several items were less than the budgeted amounts, including the Graham team's expenses, which fell about $1,200 under a budgeted figure of $19,000. No money or honorarium was paid to evangelist Graham, who receives only an annual salary from The Billy Graham Evangelistic Association.

All crusade receipts and disbursements were handled by a corporation of local men, the Billy Graham Southern Piedmont Crusade, Inc., which was dissolved after all bills had been paid and the books audited by the accounting firm, Elliott, Davis & Company. The accountant's report was published in the form of an advertisement in *The Greenville News* June 23.

Under receipts were these items:

Crusade offering, $67,801.71; pledges, $61,435.36; donations, $30,647.92; share partners, $24,432.78; sale of books and song books, less cost, $3,587.70; choir, counseling class and prayer rally offerings, $7,974.09; firm income, $273.82; miscellaneous income, $1,993.

Disbursements: Office operation, $33,193.96; Textile Hall expense, sound and lighting, parking and traffic direction, $44,-082.86; advertising, $50,102.74; Crusade team expenses and salaries, $17,829.63; nationwide television and radio ministry, $15,565.92; committee expenses, printing, supplies, postage, $24,-099.79; chairs, cost less receipts from sales, $767.05; Crusade bulletins, $10,597.03; insurance and miscellaneous items, $1,907.40.

"The spirit of giving for the work of Christ was very much in evidence throughout the campaign," said Finance Committee Chairman B. O. Thomason, Jr. "There were many highlights of the committee work, but none was more gratifying than the reception the group received from businesses and individuals who were solicited for contributions. In practically every instance a mention of the crusade would bring a cheerful response."

"I will never forget calling on the president of a local corporation who stated that all of his people were so excited by the coming of the crusade and he felt that it would mean a great deal, not only to his large industry, but to the community as well. His attitude was typical of that of a great majority of the citizens of the entire area."

Four months later, reviewing results of the crusade, Mr. Thomason said, "I am convinced, more than ever, that God has many friends in the Southern Piedmont area who needed someone like Dr. Billy Graham to ignite the spark of the Christian movement. The whole crusade renewed my feeling that there are a lot of people who really care about their spiritual life and that of their community.

"The impact of the crusade, in my humble opinion, will have a lasting effect on the Greenville community. It was an experience of a lifetime for me. I believe it was the same with thousands of other individuals, and the crusade gave our whole area a moral uplift that had not been seen for many years."

A mid-year Greenville County court report compiled by Clerk of Court Margaret W. Ross indicated a reduction in crime and the Greenville Piedmont carried a front page story about it with this headline: "Boom Times and Crusade Lower County Crime Rate." This was how staff writer Will T. Dunn wrote the lead paragraph:

> Crime has taken a marked decline in Greenville County during the past 12 months and Circuit Solicitor B. O. Thomason, Jr., has placed part of the credit on boom times and the Billy Graham Crusade.

He cited the clerk's 1966 report showing that 926 criminal cases had been disposed of in County Criminal and General Sessions courts in Greenville in the year, as compared with 1,300 cases handled during the previous twelve months. This was more than a 25 per cent decline — 348 fewer criminal cases. The biggest decrease was in the number of cases involving stealing, and a sharp decline was noted in violent crimes, murder, rape, manslaughter.

The solicitor said he thought the prosperity the area was enjoying and the Graham Crusade figured heavily in the reduction of crime.

"Being concerned daily, as solicitor of the Thirteenth Judicial Circuit, with individuals who break the law or who take the law into their own hands, it was my hope this crusade would enrich our area so much that a reduction of criminal activity might be achieved," Mr. Thomason asserted. "I believe the crusade has brought this about. Likewise, it is my conviction that many who were on the verge of breaking the law or becoming criminally inclined have not done so, due either to becoming involved in the Graham Crusade or being influenced by someone who had been in attendance."

He added; "We need more meetings of Christians from various faiths who come together under one roof and seek to serve God. I am hopeful the crusade will be only the beginning of a concerted effort by Christians in the Southern Piedmont area to work more diligently for Christ's church."

Mrs. Martha Brown, crusade office secretary, said she treasured the memory of the crusade and of working for the Lord with the fine Christian men who make up the Graham team. "They are deeply spiritual men with a genuine desire to see people find Christ," she said. "Many times we prayed together and talked over problems that arose. A man who came to the crusade office to pick up an order for materials was won for God by one of the team members. A rich spiritual blessing has been left for us as God visited our Southland in the crusade. My faith was renewed and strengthened. Throughout life I will cherish the experience the crusade brought to me."

In the choir was a soprano who had sung in revival choirs for Billy Sunday, George Cook and Mordecai Ham. Mrs. Paul Cass said she has sung in church choirs "all my life." In about 1916, she said, she was a member of a 1,500-voice choir in Baltimore singing in a Billy Sunday revival. She sang in revivals conducted by other evangelists in years following. Her son, Richard Cass, is a well-known concert pianist.

Mrs. Katherine Johnson, who operates a rural grocery store in Greenville County, sang in the crusade choir and served as a counselor. When double services were held she closed her store about 4 p.m. in order to arrive on time. Instead of losing customers by the early closing, she reported, business following the crusade was better than ever.

Mrs. Johnson gave some crusade impressions as follows: "Having the privilege of singing in the choir and being a counselor too brought unnumbered blessings to me. At the close of each service, as Mr. Graham gave his invitation, the scene would touch one's heart as the people began to move into the aisles, slowly at first, then in greater numbers. When Mr. Barrows gave the signal for counselors, I made my way down front amongst the great number coming forward, some for salvation, some for rededication. It was a thrill to witness to them for Jesus Christ. As I stood there in the great crowd, I was aware that God was surely in our midst. Just this one moment alone was worth all the effort it took to get to the services. The experience of the crusade put new joy and enthusiasm in my own life, has given me a greater desire to witness for God in my daily life."

Between services one evening Billy stood on a shaky table behind Textile Hall to express appreciation to officers handling crusade traffic. He told them he was aware of how difficult it was to direct traffic with one service following another and wanted to thank the men for their "magnificent job." To each officer he presented a copy of his book, *World Aflame*.

Capt. Lamar O. Wiggins of the Greenville District State Highway Patrol, who has planned and directed traffic flow for South Carolina's largest athletic event, the Clemson-South Carolina football game, which draws more than 40,000 spectators, was asked to compare traffic there with crusade traffic. "There are more traffic exits at the Carolina-Clemson game," he said, "but drivers to and from the crusade were more cooperative than football traffic, and that makes a big difference."

James F. McKinney of Greenville, took a week of his vacation in order to concentrate on being a crusade usher-captain.

"It was the best vacation I ever had," said Mr. McKinney, a News-Piedmont pressman. "I couldn't find a better place to go for my vacation than spending the week working for the Lord and hearing the Word. It was a great blessing for me. I had been a heavy smoker for thirty years, and in the early days of the crusade I threw my cigarettes away. I have no taste for them now."

# 16

WHEN THE SOUTHERN PIEDMONT CRUSADE WAS CARRIED ON TELE-
vision across the country, more than 800,000 people wrote to the
Billy Graham Evangelistic Association headquarters in Minneapolis for copies of *Living Gospels,* a book advertised on the
telecast. Letters were received from many others who did not
request the book.

Televised, Billy's powerful Biblical sermons promising eternal salvation and eternal life through acceptance of Jesus Christ
as Saviour found many receptive hearts.

In Greenville about 200 persons a night telephoned to seek
counseling during and following the Crusade telecasts. A caller
from Hartwell, Ga., said he had been touched by the evangelist's message and asked to be helped. "As I read a verse of
scripture to him on the telephone he made a commitment to
Christ," reported Miss Elizabeth Cridland, one of twenty-eight
counselors who took telephone calls during and following the
telecast over WFBC, Greenville. "He said that Jesus had come to
live in his heart."

Counselor John Whitman left the crusade telephone station
to comfort and pray with an 11-year-old boy who called. "If you
are not afraid to come, please come and pray with me," the boy
pleaded. "My little brother is in bed with the chicken pox."
He explained that his mother was dead and his father was in
prison.

Two divorcees with problems they couldn't solve found Christ through the telecast. A 35-year-old mother of seven who phoned was counseled by Mrs. Matthew Rabon. A young mother of three telephoning from her Georgia home told Miss Mary Beam she could not support the children and saw no solution except to send them to their father in a distant state. "I prayed and she prayed, on the telephone, and she committed her life to Christ," said Miss Beam.

Counselors continued working with the telecast inquirers in a follow-up program just as if they had gone forward in Textile Hall.

It is important that counselors memorize all of the verses of Scripture used in counseling. One Greenville counselor learned this when talking with a man who had viewed a crusade telecast in his semi-private hospital room and was to undergo serious surgery. His roommate requested the lights be turned off so he could go to sleep.

The counselor at the bedside of the surgery patient turned off the lights and continued his work for God in the darkness. He knew the verses so well he quoted them flawlessly, and soon the man facing the operation made a profession of faith. A relative who stood nearby stepped outside the room and wept for joy. Surgery revealed the patient had been stricken by a condition for which there is no known medical cure and that death likely was not far away.

The Rev. Cullen B. Crook, chairman of the Counseling and Follow-up Committee, pointed to the role of counselors and advisors in the crusade plan. "Those who came from their churches, week by week, to learn how to counsel the inquirers in the plan of salvation and how to answer many questions and problems are still in their churches doing the same thing," he said. "Their work will go on forever."

Max McGee Rice, chairman of the Crusade Visitation Committee, served also as chairman of the advisor captains during the services. In this latter capacity he went to the front when the invitation was given to be of help in special problems. "It was a great blessing to talk to many who came making decisions," he said. "I was also thrilled as I watched the counselors at work, realizing that some, for the first time, were talking with people about their relationship with God."

"As I look back on the crusade," Mr. Rice said, "I praise God for the tremendous and long-lasting benefits. Those who were born again will reap eternal blessings. Those who received counselor training will go back to their churches to be more effective than ever before. The effectiveness of preaching Christ and the Word have been demonstrated again. Those who are tempted to change our basic doctrines to suit modern man have been shown that the Gospel is still the power of God unto salvation to all who believe."

A resident of Simpsonville, S. C., wrote:

> My daughter was dating a boy who did not know God. She managed to persuade him to go to the Crusade and, in fact, he attended two services. He talked of the vastness of the crowds, the spirit prevailing during the services, the sincerity of the Crusade team members. Now he has gone into military service and he has found Christ. The Crusade in Greenville laid the foundation for this conversion.

Dr. Gordon W. Blackwell, president of Furman University, and Crusade Advisory Committee chairman, points to the crusade's wide-spread effects. "The crusade made a lasting impact on the Piedmont area," he says. "Especially were the young people helped, as many of them found new purpose for their lives and a firm mooring which is so important for adolescents. Billy Graham could speak their language and answer the questions they were asking. He expressed the feeling of many people that a world-wide spiritual awakening is the answer to the problems that beset civilization today. As I work with college youth, I see daily their need for understanding of and commitment to the religious and patriotic principles which build character. There is an upsurge of endeavor to teach youth that they have an opportunity and a responsibility to become instruments of God's purpose here on earth.

"Billy Graham has dedicated his energies to expressing his deep concern for man's need for a right relationship with God. He is not unique in his concern. He is unique in his ability to awaken the hearts and minds of millions to the reality of God's grace."

James B. Orders, Jr., crusade co-chairman, had this to say following the crusade: "Jesus said, 'Ye must be born again.'

This basic message comes out every time Billy Graham preaches. This kind of preaching requires people to change and conform to God's requirements. With the continuing breakdown in morals, muddled thinking about patriotism, and the lack of concern of man for God, we need to hear proclaimed in a loud voice, so that all will hear, 'Thus saith the Lord.' In my opinion God is using Billy Graham for this purpose."

Dr. L. D. Johnson, the general chairman, said that "Billy Graham is peculiarly effective in our time for three reasons: (1) He surely has the grace of God upon him. He is what the Bible calls a charismatic figure. He has a gift. (2) He is preaching the Gospel. He has an uncanny ability to speak to people where they are in their condition, whether it be a congregation of clergymen, a chapel filled with undergraduates, or a throng of everyday people who have come out of all kinds of situations in the world. In every case he speaks of what God has done in Christ to atone for man's sin and to bring reconciliation between man and God and man and man. (3) He is not identified with the institution of the church, although he works through the churches and believes in the church. The institutionalized church is an offense to multitudes. It is identified with irrelevance. The very fact that Billy Graham preaches outside the institutionalized church, although working through it, is part of the genius of his singular success."

In months following the crusade the World-Wide Films' release, "The Restless Ones," attracted thousands of all ages when it was shown in theaters in Greenville and Anderson and in a Spartanburg civic auditorium. The provocative movie deals with youth's rebellion in the modern world and offers an exciting answer to their problems through Christ. It interjects two episodes from the 1963 Los Angeles Crusade. In Greenville it was shown twenty-eight times in fourteen days and the Lord used it wonderfully to reach many with the Gospel that only Christ saves and gives peace.

Counselors who served during the crusade services were on hand at the film showings to aid those responding to the invitation to receive Jesus as Saviour. A girl who gave her life to Christ in the theater urged her father to see the film the next night. He attended the showing and went forward to register his decision for the Lord. The movie's influence is not restricted to youth; people of all ages rose at the invitation and went forward to be counseled.

Ray Harvey, who had charge of the showings, reported 2,650 decisions registered in the three cities, with this breakdown of statistics: Greenville, 1,230; Spartanburg, 906; Anderson, 541. On the heels of the crusade this was like "gathering up the fragments" of the harvest so that none would be lost.

To thousands beyond the great exposition hall the Graham message was told through the mass media, chiefly the newspapers. Day after day the crusade was reported by the press and made front page news in several newspapers. It was headline news in the Greenville newspapers daily. The Associated Press and United Press International moved stories on every service.

James Walker, city editor, tells of the crusade coverage in *The Greenville News,* the morning newspaper:

> Local editors played the story big. Not in the oldest editor's memory had there been such a story — that continued for so long and was, as most of them thought, worthy of such intensive coverage.
>
> Dr. Graham said from the pulpit he had seen nothing to compare with the newspaper and radio and TV coverage at Greenville.
>
> Greenville was Graham Country — in the heart of the Bible Belt a couple hour's drive from the Graham home at Montreat — and efforts to bring him had lasted nearly a decade.
>
> As thousands participated in the advance preparations, as far as a year ahead of the Crusade, it became apparent that anything connected with the Crusade would be of prime interest to readers.
>
> The flood of newspaper copy began weeks ahead. With the arrival of Dr. Graham — the night of the Monday before the Crusade opened on March 4, too late for interviews or arrival photographs — newspaper coverage reached a crescendo.
>
> *The Greenville News* used its 84-point type for across-the-page display on page 1 on the coverage of each of the 10 successive days of services. The News used 11½ pages of editorial matter, or approximately 76,000 words, and 7¾ pages of photographs.
>
> The afternoon paper, *The Greenville Piedmont,* likewise devoted hundreds of inches to photos and editorial matter.
>
> For the newspapers, as for the Graham associates, the Crusade was a "team" effort.
>
> Everybody in the shop — from reporters through desk men to printers and stereotypers and pressmen, and, of course,

photographers (who made 2,000 pictures in all) and engravers
— was in on what was, at the least, as demanding a production
job as the *News* had ever carried out.

The *News* had only about two hours between the end of the
evening service — or the last service of the day, as it turned
out — to write, edit, set into type, stereotype and print
"Graham" — as the copy was designated in each instance.

Virtually every word that was written was made available
in time for the first edition going to readers outside the county.

After the first night's deadline had been met by stretched
seconds — normally inviolate deadlines were allowed to stretch
a little those days — a harried printer said, "One down and
nine to go." But he said the words in uncommonly good spirits,
a condition that was generally to prevail through the entire
Crusade. Unquestionably, the nature of the copy had something to do with the good will throughout.

Even hardened newsmen, whom one would not ordinarily
have expected to be so enthusiastic, began to get the "feel"
of the Crusade.

Few, if any, of the thousand attending the nightly services
could have obtained the overall perspective that a team of
three photographers and half a dozen reporters acquired for
each edition of the paper.

There was too much for even someone in a choice seat in
the mammoth hall to see, hear or comprehend.

Planning almost as detailed as a "battle plan" was necessary
to carry out the coverage. The *News* city editor's assignment
memos to his staff ran to a total of more than 20 pages.

The *News* used a plane on two occasions, once for an aerial
photograph of the thousands of cars parked around "the place
where Billy's preaching" (as a headline writer captioned the
photo run six column wide on page 1), and later for a better
look at traffic conditions the day two services daily were
initiated.

Dr. Graham's messages were reported in such detail that many
readers who had heard him the night before wondered as they
read the account next morning if the reporter had not had the
benefit of a complete text of his remarks.

Dr. Graham does not speak from a prepared text, although
summaries of quotable matter often running to three or four
pages were given reporters a short time before each service.

The *News* reporter Lucille Green, took handwritten notes in
almost verbatim fashion, so that her version of the 3,500 to
4,000 word sermon ran to nearly 3,000 words including inter-
spersed "color" matter. She rushed back to the office to write

her story, but after the second service was inaugurated, dictated by direct telephone into the office.

At the outset, the Crusade press officer, Gil Stricklin, said he thought that after the first service or so, the press tables might be deserted except for the "regulars" from the local newspaper and for himself. But the lengthy tables at the front of the hall were nearly always filled with regional reporters, radio and TV reporters and photographers.

The local newspaper serviced the Associated Press with stories and photos.

The Copy desk wrote a last-night caption — "In All, 7,311 Took the Step" — over a big front page photograph of those who came forward at the next to last service.

Perhaps that summed it up better than anything else.

# 17

NOTHING OF THE MAGNITUDE AND IMPACT OF A BILLY GRAHAM
Crusade had ever come to Greenville before. That was the unan-
imous judgment of those most involved.

The sight of the massive crowd, night after night, assembled
in an attitude of spiritual inquiry and heartfelt worship, etched
itself on the memories of people attending.

On Saturday morning, the day before the last two crusade
services, the Executive Committee met for breakfast. There was
no real business before it except to rejoice in success and to
express gratitude to Billy and his team for what they had done in
the crusade. The team was classified as "All-American."

"In Billy Graham," declared A. F. Burgess, a Greenville
attorney, "we have one of the greatest advocates for the cause
of Christ I have ever heard."

The president of North Greenville Junior College, Dr. Thomas
L. Neely, said, "This crusade has made a tremendous impact
upon our youth and will have lasting effect upon their lives."

"It is the biggest 'running' story we have ever covered,"
asserted Wayne Freeman, editor of *The Greenville News* and a
member of the Executive Committee. "Dr. Graham, your influence has reached all the way from the publisher to the man

140

Wayne Freeman,
Editor, Greenville *News*
(News-Piedmont photo)

Lewis F. Brabham,
Sunday Editor of Greenville *News*
(News-Piedmont photo)

at the press . . . — We had a fine newspaper when you arrived. We have a great one now."

A Negro physician, Dr. Morris Young of Anderson, said to Billy: "After you and your team leave, just remember that I will still be on the crusade. It has meant so much to me."

The Rev. Clyde L. Ireland, rector of the Church of the Redeemer (Episcopal), said, "The crusade has added a real and new dimension to my ministry." Even before the crusade started, he added, he could feel a rising tide of concern and interest.

Dr. Cort Flint presented to the committee treasurer a $50 check given by a friend who wanted it channeled into the fund for televising the crusade.

After about an hour of testimony and expressions of gratitude, Dr. L. D. Johnson, presiding, cut off further statements from the floor and turned to Billy for closing remarks.

The evangelist, a glowing witness for Christ as always, told the committee that he had been overwhelmed at what had happened in the crusade and that it had far exceeded all expectations.

"When people are working and praying together, God pours out a blessing," Billy said. "To get the church membership mobilized is of tremendous importance."

He quoted Dr. John S. Bonnell of New York as saying that 65 counselors from his church, Fifth Avenue Presbyterian, served during the 1957 crusade and that even when the crusade had ended they kept on working and bringing people within the influence of the church.

Billy stressed the importance of follow-up and a continual program of evangelism. He predicted that five years later there would be people in the area holding places of religious leadership who would date their awakening to decisions made in the crusade. To take a public stand for God, he added, can be a vital step in a person's life and growth in the faith.

"With all our hearts," he said in closing, "let us give God the praise for what has happened during these days."

The final services of the crusade were held on what might have been labeled "Thank You Day." Tributes were paid many whose efforts contributed to the success of the undertaking.

In his closing message, Billy pleaded with his listeners to "repent" as he preached on "The Great Judgment Day."

"Have you repented?" he asked. "If you haven't you will perish. Judgment Day is already set and you'll be there."

Showing no signs of the strain that two-a-day services imposed, the evangelist paced the speaker's platform with God's message. This was the final challenge of a record-setting campaign against forces of evil.

"I am asking you to decide for Christ, to let Him come into your heart and change your life," he said in earnest and compelling tones. "His forgiveness will wipe all your sins from His memory — only you will remember them. Jesus bought these sins when He hung on the cross. He took your sins and my sins and granted us forgiveness, if we only have faith to believe on Him.

"God commandeth all men everywhere to repentance. God is not suggesting we repent of our sins; He commands it. Penitence simply means that you turn away from your prejudice, pride, lust, greed, jealousy, hatred, to a new dimension of living found in the person of Jesus Christ."

Many consciences were touched by the rapier-like words of the evangelist, urging, pleading for all to come face to face with God. Nearly one thousand people went forward on this climactic day to register decisions for Christ.

The torch was passed and the momentous crusade moved into history, leaving behind indelible and joyous memories. The crusade message that "Christ died for our sins" would flow from Textile Hall into the hearts and lives of thousands, in the freshly stimulated atmosphere of hundreds of churches, thousands of homes, professional offices and places of business.

In the crusade audiences one was impressed with the atmosphere of good will and love which was so manifest, the feeling of oneness drawing residents of a broad region, white and Negro, executive and laborer, closer together.

New spiritual and moral development and growth was kindled in a section of the nation that is coming to the fore with its great industrial and business expansion.

Greenville towered as a propelling force, a "launching pad," for Billy's preparation for his next major mission, the incalculable

Crusade crowds  (News-Piedmont photos)

challenge of London,[1] ten weeks after the Southern Piedmont Crusade. What happened in his southeastern homeland sky-rocketed him into a re-invigorated state of health and mind, refreshing his spirit for his month-long summer religious foray into England.

The Greenville campaign and its subsequent telecast by some 300 stations gave residents across the nation a new insight into an area of the South that is often misunderstood and misjudged, or too harshly judged, for its shortcomings, both imaginary and real.

White and Negro worshiped side by side and sang together as they did decades ago — and not a single unpleasant incident marred the interracial crusade. It was a significant religious event in the heart of Dixie, a bold pioneering move to bring together divergent feelings and differing heritages.

The lucid result was a wave of new strength of race relations that reached out from the hall far beyond the borders of South Carolina. There was integrated counseling, as well as mixed seating and singing, without noticeable effects. Race-conscious-ness, which has been accentuated and aggravated nationwide, was submerged in a common purpose.

In a year that brought racial clashes and rioting to cities of the North, Midwest and West Coast as well as other parts of the South, the Southern Piedmont Crusade produced the san-guine experience of racial harmony and understanding. To those who know the region best, this was no surprise.

People of both races went forward at all services and stood together in the circle of the committed to be counseled. "I watched them in thanksgiving to God that this was happening in the South," Billy said. "Once again it underscored that there is no color bar before the cross."

Billy's influence in behalf of racial oneness in Christian wor-ship has long been felt. Even before the Supreme Court decision against school segregation, he laid down his own working rule against it in crusades and meetings.

---

[1]The London campaign turned out to be a success from all stand-points and eclipsed records set when Billy preached there for three months in 1954. More than one million people heard him in Earl's Court and by closed-circuit television in other cities in England. Decisions for Christ during the campaign numbered 42,487.

"There is only one possible solution to the race problem, and that is a vital experience with Jesus Christ on the part of both races," he said. "In Christ the middle wall of partition has been broken down. There is no Jew, no Gentile — no black, white, yellow, or red. We could be one great brotherhood in Jesus Christ.

"However, until we come to recognize Him as the Prince of Peace and receive His love in our hearts, the racial tensions will increase, racial demands will become more militant, and a great deal of blood will be shed."

Graham meetings are open to everyone without qualification, regardless of time or place. Billy knows the problems and frustrations of minorities, he recognizes their crying need for expression and opportunity, and he works constantly to help speed their deliverance from prejudice. But he opposes rioting in the name of civil rights, mass demonstrations and other so-called non-violent disobedience of law.

Mrs. Vera Starks of Greenville, who is Negro, spoke of the Crusade's effect on race relations.

"There was no resentment in the crusade hall," she said. "I dropped my coat in the aisle one night and a white person picked it up and smiled at me. I didn't see a smug look on anybody. I believe with all of my heart that our city and area will be a better place for Billy Graham coming."

She went forward at the crusade, she said, "because I wanted to rededicate my life to Him — and to carry some of this spirit back to my church."

Dr. J. Guy Douglas, a Negro dentist of Greenville, viewed the crusade as "one of the greatest things that ever happened in our city and section of the country. Its spiritual blessing to the community has been immeasurable," he said, "and it revealed that colored and white people can come together and worship without prejudice."

He attended five of the services and sat with white people, as did hundreds of other Negroes. "I had a seat near the front each night," he continued. "Everyone was attentive and courteous and there were no distinctions as we worshiped together. So far as I know, people were not race conscious at the crusade. I went there as a person, among other people, to hear Billy Graham and to participate in the service. The crusade had a good effect on race relations in our area and I believe that its benefits will continue to be felt in the future."

One of the heart-warming experiences of the crusade, Dr. Johnson said, was "the counseling of a Negro boy, about 13 years of age, by a white boy, whose age I learned was 14. One could see the open Bible between them during the counseling. The young counselor was the son of a pastor in another county."

Negroes served on all committees from the policy-making Executive Committee through the entire organization. The Executive Committee secretary was Harrison Rearden, a Negro insurance executive.

The non-racial crusade stands as proof, Mr. Rearden said, that whites and Negroes can meet together amicably and stand together with a common purpose, even in the deep South. "There is no denying," he said, "the crusade proved to the public that it can be done.

"It has long been my conviction," he continued, "that if we can come together in an attitude of sharing spiritually, then the solution to problems of race will follow. The Southern Piedmont Crusade may have been a long step toward that end.

"As white people sat by colored people, singing together, praying and worshiping together, the thought occurred to me, 'Why can't this give birth to a new day and a new life?' "

"In the Greenville area, there seems to be a spirit of genuine friendship in many quarters, and we are heartened by this," he said. "This attitude of better understanding has to some extent boosted the morale of the people of the city. What the future holds we cannot say, but we are encouraged, and much of this can be attributed to the crusade."

From the beginning it was plain that there would be no color barrier in the crusade. "What we did, from the first prayer for guidance in planning to the last benediction and thanksgiving, we did together," Dr. Johnson related. "Every effort was made to remove all doubt in the minds of Negro Christians that this might be another 'loaded' proposition.

"We approached the entire question of the need for a spiritual awakening from the standpoint of our common need — not white needs or Negro needs," Dr. Johnson said. "We made it plain that we were not seeking to promote anyone or anything except Jesus Christ as Lord. Therefore, the question of segregation-integration was irrelevant. We didn't ask, 'Is this man white or black?' We asked, 'Does he know Christ and can he help others to know Him?'"

"In all fairness, it should be said that we had something less than our hoped-for response from Negroes in certain areas of the effort, particularly in the training of counselors. However, even in this difficult work there were many fine Negro Christians who participated," he continued. "As far as I know there was not a single ugly incident that had racial overtones. On the other hand, I witnessed many heart-warming expressions of Christian love and acceptance by both races toward each other during the crusade. I cannot but believe that the spirit will leave a lasting deposit in Greenville and the Piedmont."

The Rev. David C. Francis, a Greenville Negro minister, thinks the crusade's impact on race relations will continue to be felt. "In various functions, in a spirit of genuine cooperation and respect for each other, white and colored friends are working together in our city," he said. "The Billy Graham Crusade was one of the fostering influences in this encouraging result. Greenville has never had the disturbances, the wide-spread hatred and racial strife troubling some cities, and I believe that we can expect race relations to be even better in the future." Mr. Francis is pastor of Springfield Baptist Church, which has been the scene of many civil rights rallies.

Their moral fibers strengthened by participation in the crusade, many people took a new grip on their faith in Christ. Public officials from mayors to the Governor of the state, leaders in numerous fields and professions, pastors and thousands of "just plain Christians" united in the crusade to add new pages to the history of Greenville and South Carolina.

"One thing that helped the most was the cooperation of everyone in the community in their efforts to put the crusade across," commented Dr. Johnson. "The spirit of the people exceeded all expectations. The whole area will feel the impact of the crusade, in countless ways, for years to come."

As the crusade drew to a close and the time neared for the Graham team to move on to another mission, the evangelist told the clergy of the area that the work of soul-winning in the Southern Piedmont was being left in their hands to continue.

Solemnly, clearly, Billy said, "It is to them (the clergy) we now hand the torch — and it is my prayer that when the last sermon has been given, the last song is sung, and the last prayer prayed, and the great crowds melt into the night, that the results of this crusade will last in the hearts of many."

The clear evidence since has been that they have — and will.

# 18

## FAVORITE VERSES

Billy Graham has many favorite Bible verses. This is one of his best loved:

*Philippians 1:6:* Being confident of this very thing, that he which hath begun a good work in you will perform it until the day of Jesus Christ.

Here are favorite verses of some of the other Graham team members:

Grady Wilson
*II Corinthians 5:17:* Therefore if any man be in Christ, he is a new creature: old things are passed away; behold, all things become new.

Howard Jones
*Jeremiah 33:3:* Call unto me, and I will answer thee, and shew [show] thee great and mighty things, which thou knowest not.

**T. W. Wilson**
*Romans 8:28:* And we know that all things work together for good to them that love God, to them who are the called according to his purpose.

**Abdul Akbar Haqq**
*I Timothy 1:15:* This is a faithful saying, and worthy of all acceptation, that Christ Jesus came into the world to save sinners; of whom I am chief.

**Leighton Ford**
*II Corinthians 5:19-20:* To-wit, that God was in Christ, reconciling the world unto himself, not imputing their trespasses unto them; and hath committed unto us the word of reconciliation.

Now then we are ambassadors for Christ, as though God did beseech you by us: we pray you in Christ's stead, be ye reconciled to God.

**Cliff Barrows**
*Psalm 98:1:* O sing unto the Lord a new song; for he hath done marvelous things: his right hand, and his holy arm, hath gotten him the victory.

**John Lenning**
*Phillippians 4:13:* I can do all things through Christ which strengtheneth me.

**Willis G. Haymaker**
*II Chronicles 7:14:* If my people, which are called by my name, shall humble themselves, and pray, and seek my face, and turn from their wicked ways; then will I hear from heaven, and will forgive their sin, and will heal their land.

# 19

## CRUSADE QUOTES

Even if the Southern Piedmont Crusade were to be canceled today, this area would have achieved permanent benefit.
— *Billy Graham* at pre-crusade news conference

I ask you to be here every night, I plan to be here every night.
— *Billy Graham* to ushers, choir members, counselors at pre-crusade rehearsal

Nobody is here by accident.
— *Billy Graham* at first crusade service

The auditorium was filled before the service started and that was our goal.
— *Charles W. Scales*, chairman of Crusade Traffic Committee

There's one thing I regret since I became a Christian. I've let God down so many times, but He's never let me down one time. You just have to look up, to reach up, and He's there ready to help you.
— *Steve Sloan*, Atlanta Falcon quarterback

I know what Christ means to me. I think Billy Graham is the best one to give Christ to teenagers.
> — *Mike Fair,* University of South Carolina Gamecock quarterback

We are now near the halfway point. This is one of the greatest Monday night services I have experienced in the world.
> — *Billy Graham*

This crusade is a once-in-a-lifetime chance, for Billy Graham has been given by God the gift of being a prophet.
> — *Dr. L. D. Johnson,* crusade chairman

God has trusted Billy Graham and he has never let God down.
> — *Willis Haymaker,* veteran crusade director

Sexual immorality is a greater threat to our national security tonight than is Red China.
> — *Billy Graham*

Some are here out of curiosity, but most are searching for the way, the truth and the life.
> — *Richard Lyons,* Toccoa Falls (Ga.) Bible Institute student

I believe that within the next few days we will be able to see an historic spiritual impact that will have a far-reaching effect on the entire Southeastern part of our country.
> — *Billy Graham* on fourth day of crusade

Isn't it wonderful what God can do?
> — *Ethel Waters,* crusade singer

As prosecuting attorney in General Sessions Court, I know that more than 50 per cent of the crimes in the judicial circuit are committed by persons between 16 and 23 years of age. Reaching masses of young people, as Mr. Graham did last night, is a great blessing.
> — *B. O. Thomason, Jr.,* court solicitor and crusade finance chairman

Impossible things can be done, not because of your faith, but because of the object of your faith.

— *Cliff Barrows* at hotel luncheon during crusade

If anybody saw me kissing a lovely, beautiful woman who looks like a teenager backstage last night, that was my wife who was here for the first service.

— *Billy Graham*

One of our major problems is the mass of people who want to see and talk with Billy Graham. He is known far and wide and there are so many people wanting to talk with him. Many times he would like to see them, but his strength and schedule have to be considered. He is just one man and there is only so much he can do.

— *Gil Stricklin*, Graham public relations assistant

I have always been able to see the audience before, but in the crusade hall I couldn't tell where the audience began and where it ended. It was all around.

— *Myrtle Hall*, soloist

I think she is wonderful. God has given her a voice that has beauty and a wholesome quality. She is beautiful inside and out.

— *Ethel Waters*, referring to young singer Myrtle Hall

There is no obvious explanation, except God is working. If I was here every night, I would be torn emotionally, limb from limb. It is all of Christianity, in a capsule.

— *Dr. Marc Weersing*, president, Presbyterian College, Clinton, S. C.

To them (the clergy) we now hand the torch. And it is my prayer that when the last sermon has been given, the last song is sung, the last prayer is prayed, and the great crowds melt into the night, that the results of this crusade will last in the hearts of many.

— *Billy Graham* at final service

I'm dropping the "re" part of my title. I'm just tired.
— *Col. Clifford E. Singleton*, U. S. Army retired, chairman of Crusade Usher Committee, after final service

Nothing has ever thrilled me so much as the tremendous response in the Southern Piedmont Crusade. God was there, and the results of the crusade will be seen more and more as time goes on — in the community, in the churches, in the lives of individuals.
— *Willis G. Haymaker*, crusade associate director

Sherwood Wirt

Stan Mooneyham

Forest Layman

Walter Smyth

Miss Ethel Waters and Miss Myrtle Hall (News-Piedmont photo)

Tedd Smith                    Don Hustad

Leighton Ford

Hank Beukema

Howard O. Jones

John Lenning

Abdul Akbar Haqq